THIS SIDE O

DOOR

By

John E. Hosier

Dedication

To

Georgie

Suzi

Nancy

Isabel

Ethan

Fliss

Maddy

Acknowledgements

My thanks to Amazon Publishing Agency (APA) for their help and support as I prepared this book for publication.

They have been very patient in handling many revisions and corrections and also in designing the front cover, which really captures in picture form the hope that I express in telling my story.

Particular thanks to Mathew.... who helped me get back on track when it seemed that my manuscript had gotten lost somewhere, out there, in the mysterious way that documents sometimes disappear when you press the Send button.

About the Author

Born in London, John Hosier has always had a great love for the sea. This probably began because of holidays in Cornwall, which he enjoyed from the age of eight, and forever gave him a love of swimming and surfing. At the age of eighteen, he 'went to sea' as he joined the Merchant Navy for three years. Having left the Navy and followed by a period of study at Spurgeons's College, he became a Pastor in several different churches. Also, he spent a few years teaching at Moorlands Bible College. Every time he moved, it was always to a venue near the sea. Retirement has been spent near the sea in Cape Town, South Africa, and then in Bournemouth and, more recently, in what is probably a final house move to Poole, where his study overlooks the harbour.

At the time of writing his story, he has been married to Sue for fifty-five years, and their immediate family comprises two sons and seven grandchildren. In retirement, John has continued to preach, teach, write a blog, swim, and enjoy the beach.

Table of Contents

Introduction

I understand a paradox to be an explainable contradiction. There are many paradoxes in the Bible.

One that I have found particularly helpful in understanding my own life is when Paul says: 'We commend ourselves in every way:.....sorrowful, yet always rejoicing.' (2 Corinthians 6:1). I can absolutely identify with that. There are many things that I am really sorrowful about, such as the state of the world and the state of the church, even without going into detail. At the very same time, I can feel full of joy at the wonder of God's love, the experience of his grace, and the hope for all that is to come.

One of the best-known sayings of Jesus is also put in the form of a paradox. 'I am the resurrection and the life. The one who believes in me will live, even though they die; and whoever lives by believing in me will never die.' (John 11:25, 26). Well, do you die or don't you die? But a Believer can resolve the paradox. I often try an illustration to bring out the meaning. I tell my hearers to imagine that they only ever live in a large house. They never see or go outside; all their life is spent in this house. During their life, they occasionally move from one room to another and stay there for a time. Some rooms are very luxurious, and you have a great time there. Others are dilapidated and uncomfortable, and it's not a great experience staying in those. But mostly, the rooms are reasonable, and you're happy enough to be there. During your life, you become aware of a back door to the house, and sometimes you wonder what is on the other side. Then, one day, you find yourself being drawn towards that door, and you can't resist moving towards it. Suddenly the door swings open, and you are compelled to go through it, and then, for the first time, you see blue sky, trees, green grass, and a beautiful wide lake – everything is different. I say the death of a Believer will be like that. One day

1

we will have to go through a door that we can call death, but on the other side, it will be all gain, all beauty, and we'll be alive in a dimension beyond anything we have experienced before.

This book is about my life on this side of that door. There have been the good times and the bad times, but often my life has been such that the room has been reasonable, and I've been happy enough to be there. I'm sure many could read my story and conclude I've had a very good life. And, yes, I would agree with that. But there have been times of worry and sorrow. Family members and friends get ill and die. Tragedies occur that have impinged on my life in some way. I remember once preaching to the Brighton Church when I was an elder there and saying to them, "some of you may look at my life and think I've been very fortunate compared to some of you, and that may be true." But I added, "I've had my times when I could scream with the frustrations that I've felt or disappointments that have hit me." Sorrowful but always rejoicing.

This book is a biography, and therefore it gives an overview of my personal history. I also make quite a lot of comments on what I have experienced, so it is not just a history; it contains how I think about things as well.

I had considered writing my life story for a few years. About a year before I wrote this book, I worked out a detailed outline and kept it beside me on my desk. I often had the feeling that I ought to start writing it out in full, but then I reckoned no one was going to publish it, so do I just make a photocopy and leave it in a folder for anyone in the family who wants to read it? But in October 2022, I had an annual meet-up with my friend Nigel Ring. We'd had been work colleagues for all the twenty-three years that I was a church elder in Brighton. We now live two hours apart, so once a year, we each drive for about an hour to have lunch together at a

Garden Centre (no expense spared). On this occasion, he handed me his autobiography '80 Not Out', and as soon as he did, I realised it was self-published. I wondered why I hadn't thought of doing that, but it was the provocation for me to get on and write this book.

I have received a great deal of help from Georgina, my eldest granddaughter, who has patiently worked through and edited the whole manuscript. I've learnt a lot from her as she has wielded her metaphorical red pencil and adopted a fairly free 'slash and burn' approach to my writing. I discovered that I use far too many adverbs, and some of my sentences are flowery and wordy. I have been much corrected, but if there are still sentences that still need correction or pruning, that is my fault and not that of my granddaughter.

A huge thank you to my wife, who has had to suffer constant references by me to what I was writing without being allowed to read it until I had finished. I am sure that she is very relieved not to hear me say again, 'well, that's another chapter finished.' Inevitably, though, when I checked some facts with her as the writing continued, she often could direct my course on some details.

So many people have had an impact on my life, and most of them won't be named in this book.

There are a lot of names that I do mention, but so many more that aren't given. I am grateful to everyone, but more than grateful that there is one name above every name, and his name is Jesus.

I hope my appreciation of his grace in my life will be clear in this story.

Chapter 1

The Early Years

I regret having talked so little to my parents about memories of their early lives. Because of it, I know nothing at all about my great-grandparents. Talking, however, would have been difficult with my father. Always being a very reserved personality, it took me years to work out that he was born outside of marriage, a reason that led to his being brought up by his grandmother. Though I never talked to him about this, I learned from others that he grew up in great poverty in Kentish Town in North London. He once drove me past the small terraced house he lived in as a boy. I imagine that when he was young, it was virtually a slum, but over the course of time, with the extraordinary uplift of prices in that part of London, it became worth hundreds of thousands of pounds. Much like the house, his life was something of a rags-to-riches story. Aged 14, he joined a building firm in Kentish Town as the 'tea-boy'. He retired from there 51 years later as Managing Director, by which time he was living in a large house in Finchley and the owner of a second home in Newquay. This bungalow in Cornwall was the home that my parents lived in towards the end of their lives.

My mother was a beauty. I know that one can hold exaggerated opinions of one's own family, but she really was, and she was always very conscious of her looks. She told me she married my father at the age of 17 - straight from school, I supposed, and that I was born when she was 19. When she died at the age of 81 (or so I thought), I accessed my parents' personal documents only to discover from her birth and marriage certificates that she was, in fact, 84, that she married at the age of 20 and gave birth to me aged 22.

She liked to be considered younger than she was though that was hardly necessary. Even in old age, she retained her looks, and people could not believe she was anywhere near 81, let alone 84. This did, however, explain why she seemed so embarrassed when we gave her a special present for her '80th' birthday. So where was she during the missing years of 17 to 20? Those were war years, and we eventually worked out that she had been employed in an armaments factory in Swindon, but it would have been rather below her dignity to admit it!

I was born in London in 1944 and evacuated to Newcastle with my mother until the end of the war. After that, and until age 10, we lived in a very simple end-of-terrace house in the non-posh part of Highgate near the Archway Road that ran towards central London. In 2022 I identified this house on Google maps and Zoopla. It still stands with a conservatory added on and was valued at a total mind-blowing 1.6 million pounds! The only explanation I can give for this extraordinary value is the convenience of being near central London.

Looking back to my earliest years, I have very little memory of anything until I started attending a Junior School in Highgate at the age of five. I would describe my childhood as secure rather than happy. Neither parent was particularly affectionate, and my father always seemed rather stern. When I was four, my sister was born, but we always attended different schools. At the age of eight, I was transferred to a boy's Preparatory School in Muswell Hill called Norfolk House, a bus ride away from home, which was distinguished by the fact that the pupils wore orange caps and blazers. Apparently, some years before I arrived, a group of boys were causing trouble on a local street, and it was reported that they came from Norfolk House. This proved incorrect, and the Headmaster felt that a good way to make sure his boys could be clearly identified was to dress them in orange. Also, we wore short trousers, and as we were there until the age of thirteen, this requirement caused friction with some parents as they felt that their very grown-up-looking sons should not be forced to remain in shorts.

The Headmaster, a severe individual quite free in applying the slipper, used to clear his throat loudly before entering a classroom, warning of his approach, and would then always find the class in good order. The school was cold in winter to the point where one teacher allowed us to wear gloves. The Head, however, wouldn't tolerate this, the teacher was quite literally told to get on his bike, and we never saw him again. I doubt that would happen today.

Neither, I suspect, would the (Physical Education) PE teacher be allowed to hold a stick in his hand and deliver a sharp whack to the legs of boys who were not keeping up with the exercises. Despite this, it was a happy enough school, there was no bullying, and I enjoyed the football and cricket and the daily bottle of milk supplied in those post-war years by the government to all school pupils.

I did reasonably well academically and passed the Common Entrance Exam, which was required to get me into a Public School (which was, in fact, private and fee-paying) and was sent to Mercer's School near High Holborn in central London. By this time, we had moved to a new house, built by my father's company, in North Finchley, and so my journey required a one-mile walk to a tube station, a journey down the Northern Line to Tottenham Court Road, where I changed to the Central Line before reaching my destination. However, this didn't last long. Mercers was a small school, and it was in financial difficulties, which led to its closure a year after I joined. So I was transferred to another all-boys school called Haberdashers in Cricklewood until that was rebuilt and rehoused on a brand new site in Elstree, to which I transferred again.

Academically I was now out of my depth. I was never very good at maths, and most boys had joined the school at eleven and studied science for two years before I arrived. I'd never had a science lesson before I joined at thirteen, and I never caught up. However, I passed six 'O' levels (including maths after some extra tuition) and went on to study 'A' levels, but then halfway through left school to join the Merchant Navy.

Conversion

From a young age, I attended afternoon Sunday School at Kentish Town Mission. My father had gone there also as a young boy, though I don't know the history of that. He had grown up in the congregation there and remained going even when moving to Highgate and then further away to Finchley. In fact, for some years during my childhood, he went to Sunday morning and evening as well as teaching in the Sunday School on Sunday afternoon. This caused some tension with my mother, who really leaned towards the High Church of England. For some years, while we were in Finchley, she attended an Anglican Church in Barnet on a Sunday morning but would sometimes go with my father to Kentish Town in the evening.

Kentish Town Mission was an old-fashioned gospel hall with a smaller morning meeting and a larger evening gathering at which the gospel would be preached. Those styles of fellowships usually transitioned into calling themselves Evangelical Churches, and sure enough, 'The Mission' in time became Kentish Town Evangelical Church and called a full-time pastor. It was there at the age of 10, and I always remember it was the first day of Spring; I consciously committed my life to Christ towards the end of a Sunday School meeting. When invited to pray, I simply said,

'Lord, make me strong.' As for many who come to faith early in life, there were to be plenty of bumps along the road, but I certainly date my conversion to that date.

At about the same time, Billy Graham came to the UK for his famous 1954 Haringey Crusade. Despite having initially come for a few weeks, Dr Graham stayed three months, at which time he made headline news. His final meeting filled Wembley Stadium, and from that time, his gift as an evangelist became known worldwide. I certainly went to some of those meetings. The one that sticks in my mind was organised especially for children and young people and included a guest appearance by the film star Roy Rogers, a cowboy, and his horse Trigger. Roy was an evangelical Christian – I can't speak for the horse!

Over the years, my parent's church-going evolved and included visits to Westminster Chapel, Muswell Hill Baptist Church and another Baptist Church in Central London. But from age twelve, I switched to attending North Finchley Baptist Church on Sunday mornings and evenings, as well as Finchley Crusader Class on Sunday afternoons. The latter was where Cliff Richard was involved for some time.

The Baptist Church I attended was certainly not evangelical, but it had a thriving youth work. This was largely fed by a Boys Scout troop and Girls Guide Company that also met at the Church building and where all the leaders were in the congregation. This was where I first met a young teenage girl called Susan Walker, who -some years later- became my wife. Her claim has always been that she was first attracted by my knees; for then, Scouts always wore shorts. I mention this because of a rather interesting incident that occurred many years later, as I'll make clear.

As it happened, we were both baptised at the same meeting; on my fifteenth birthday. Sue came from a non-church-going family but was invited to a baptism service by the girl who lived next door. At that service, Sue knew that God had a claim on her life, she joined the church youth group, and then, having come to faith, we were baptised on the same day.

I was still a member of that church and half way through my 'A' level studies when I decided to begin a career in the Merchant Navy as a Navigating Officer, joining the BP Oil Tanker Company in February 1962.

In The Navy

I joined the BP fleet because, in those days, it was the largest merchant fleet in the UK and therefore seemed to offer the potential for a career that started with training as a cadet officer but could eventually lead to being a captain of a huge oil tanker. As a cadet with no background or experience of the sea or ships at all, I discovered that I was regarded as a fairly lowly species! Every morning when at sea, there was one hour of guided self-study leading to an exam which, if passed, meant you would become a third officer.

But most of the time, you were just used as cheap labour. When at sea, that mostly involved cleaning and painting the accessible parts of the ship that were constantly showing signs of rust due to the salty water. Visits to a port to load or discharge oil were usually quite brief, and 8 hours of each 24 would be spent helping with the loading/unloading process, which as a cadet, usually meant measuring how much oil was in the tanks. Getting time ashore meant skimping on sleep if one was going to see or do much at all. However, it wasn't unusual for the ship to need some repairs, which could lead to longer times in port and more opportunities to explore.

My highlights from this time include visiting a port in Sweden. The vessel I was on was the first to arrive after winter, and we followed an icebreaker ship while sailing along motorbikes racing on the ice right beside us. I made a couple of trips to New York and went up the Empire State building, then the tallest building in the world. For some reason, I often seemed to be in Antwerp and got to know the city quite well. On another occasion, I was in a port in Columbia with some other crew from the ship, and we hired a taxi which I believed was taking us to a restaurant. It took me some time to realise that we had, in fact, arrived at a Brothel, this only dawning on me as we drank our pre-dinner drinks (so I thought) when a group of girls were lined up in front of us. I fled, got into another taxi, and managed to do some sightseeing in the city.

My faith wobbled a bit at this time, but I had joined the Merchant Navy Christian Fellowship, and on being honest in a letter to a correspondent in the group about my struggles, he wrote faithfully to help me continue on course. While I was grateful for his encouragement, I must admit I was beginning to look forward more to letters that might be waiting at the next port from a certain Susan Walker. There was, of course, no email in those days. Sue had discovered through a conversation that I was feeling a bit lonely at sea and decided to write to me. When I came home on leave with a little money in my pocket, it was she I wanted to ask out on a date. West Side Story was showing in a cinema in central London – would she like to see it with me? She would. To this day, I hold a vivid memory of her stepping off a bus near Golders Green tube station, where we had agreed to meet. Still a teenager, very pretty, her lovely blond hair blowing in the breeze, dressed very nicely for a first date. I probably fell in love at that moment. Our romance began.

There are three events which occurred during my brief career at sea that have remained strongly in my mind. One was the Cuban missile crisis which was developing while I was at home on leave. The Russians were sending a ship carrying nuclear warheads to be installed in Cuba, just 90 miles off the American mainland. John Kennedy, President of the United States, told the Russians he would not allow the ship to dock in Cuba. There was a tense international crisis when the possibility of a nuclear war between America and Russia seemed very real. The world held its breath. For some reason, I can't recall; it was during the peak of the crisis that my Company required me to attend a lecture in Central London, which I think was at the Methodist Central Hall in Westminster. I sat through the afternoon wondering what was going on between Russia and America. At one point, the lecture was illustrated by a film of missiles being fired, something which I couldn't help but worry might be happening for real between the two super powers as I sat there. I came out of the lecture and passed a newspaper stand with a poster declaring: Russian ship turns back. I was extremely relieved, as were a few billion other people!

The second memory is of the run-up to Christmas one year when I was on a tanker in a dry dock in Cardiff where it was undergoing maintenance and repairs. To have a ship in dry dock over Christmas with no work being done would cost a lot for nothing, so the Company was determined that we should sail on the day before Christmas Eve. As we set out, the December mist turned into a thick fog. I was on the Bridge of the ship at the time as we were being towed towards the open sea by two tugs. Suddenly the captain, who was looking at the radar screen, shouted; there's a ship ahead of us! He told me to instruct the engine room to put the ship into reverse, but as the two tugs slipped their ropes to move away from us, we ploughed straight into a cargo vessel, albeit at slow speed. We were then towed back into the dry dock to get the damage repaired. I had some time with my parents that Christmas before being transferred to another ship. I had to give a statement to an official from the Company about the accident, which was quite intense as the captain was also present. I told it exactly as I remembered it, including how the captain had seen the other ship on the radar just before the collision. He point-blank denied it, and I was left feeling rather foolish and having to admit I might have misunderstood. I never did work that one out!

The third and most significant event happened on November 9th 1963. As a cadet, I had to write a journal about life on board the ship, which the captain would read and comment on once a month. I've kept that journal, and this is how I wrote about that November morning:

A white flash of light:- BANG and at 4.10 yesterday morning, I was thrown onto the deck amongst a hundred splinters of glass and china. Immediately the ringing of alarm bells, and I grab my life jacket and rush out of my cabin onto the deck. We were listing badly to starboard, and the air was filled with acrid smoke.

I was on a ship called the British Industry, and it had just suffered the biggest explosion on any BP Oil Tanker since the Second World War. It had taken place in one of the ship's oil tanks which had been emptied of crude oil but was full of gas after being unloaded. During a time of tank cleaning, somehow, a spark had been ignited and reacted with the gas to cause the explosion. The ship limped into Bombay (now Mumbai), where repairs were made, but because the damage was so serious, we were later given orders to sail to Naples for a full repair job, and the crew were flown home. This was a life-changing event for me. I realised I could very easily have been killed in that accident, and I began to wonder what did God really want me to do with my life? After considerable prayer and thought, I believed that God would have me serve his church as a pastor. I was a member of a Baptist Church, and so the logical thing to do was apply to a Baptist Training College. This wasn't a quick process, and I went back to sea for one more voyage before resigning as a cadet and preparing for four years of training at Spurgeon's College in London.

Chapter 2

College Life

Spurgeon's College in London was founded in 1856 by the great Victorian Preacher and Pastor of the Metropolitan Tabernacle in London, C H Spurgeon. He drew thousands to hear him preach every Sunday and built the largest mega-church in the world at that time. Originally called The Pastor's College, its name was later changed in honour of its founder. In my college days then and still today, in 2023, it is based on a campus near South Norwood in South London.

To study for a Bachelor of Divinity degree at the college, I needed a minimum of two 'A' levels. Of course, I had left school before completing those to enter the Navy, so when I finished my last voyage and returned home, I found a job in the Treasury Department of Friern Barnet Town Hall in North London and studied for the 'A' levels in the evening via a correspondence course. I managed to pass the two I needed after a year and was accepted into Spurgeon's in the Autumn of 1965.

By this time, Sue and I had been going out together for a while. Over the Christmas period, at the end of my first term, we became engaged. Our engagement was for two and a half years - not something I'd recommend, on which I'll comment later.

Most students did a four-year course of study at Spurgeon's, taking either the BD or a Diploma in Theology. The college was small, with an average of sixteen students each year (eighteen in my year). Across the four intake groups, there were about sixty-five students, almost all of whom were single men, but there were a few who were married and lived outside of the college. Many of us began our studies at the age of twenty-one and were then leading a church by the age of twenty-five.

The College

Some years later, I left the Baptist denomination, but I've always felt it important not to spurn one's roots. I still feel very grateful for my years at Spurgeon's and for all I learned at that time. Inevitably, however, there was the good and the not-so-good.

The College Principal was Dr George Beasley-Murray, a scholar, an excellent communicator, and the author of several books, including an important commentary on John's gospel in the Word Biblical Commentary series. His lectures on John were of high calibre and eagerly attended. He was committed to teaching the Kingdom of God, but somehow I never connected with it. Years later, I happened to meet him at Brighton station, and we travelled together on a train to London. We talked about college days (should I still call him sir, or was it now George?), and by this time, an understanding of the Kingdom of God had become enormously important in my own ministry. I mentioned this to him, along with the fact that it wasn't something I had grasped while at Spurgeon's. I must say he was very gracious in his reply: *there is a time for seeing things.*

As for other staff and classes, the Old Testament lecturer began his teaching role as I entered college and was a real enthusiast for the subject. New Testament Greek was challenging for some of the students though I took to it fairly well. The lecturer for this was a great preacher, clearly with good pastoral experience behind him. However, he was easily distracted – for which we enjoyed his teaching. The theology lectures were dull, comprising the same notes that the lecturer had obviously been churning out monotonously for years. Church History was a joke. Years later, I taught Early Church History myself within the NewFrontiers family of churches. I reckon that I got more content across in 2 days than I received from our lectures in Spurgeon's in 2 years. On reflection, the situation should have been addressed, but everything was very formal then. On the whole, students didn't complain, and we addressed the lecturers as 'sir', while we, as students, were always addressed as 'Mr'.

I think that the main weakness of the teaching programme was that it was too academically driven. The award of the degree was the main aim, or at least that is how it seemed. We had no real teaching on church leadership, though we picked up some useful input through casual contact with the lecturers. There were some lectures on what was called 'Pastoralia', which were a kind of a mishmash of information on how to do funerals, lead church meetings and advice not to refuse cups of tea when doing pastoral visitation. These lectures were given by the college administrator and lacked any sense of vision for leading a church. I've reflected much over the years on pastoral and leadership training programmes, particularly because four years at Spurgeon's was repeatedly referred to as training for the Baptist ministry. But it wasn't, and I really trained for the Baptist ministry when I began to lead a church and then learnt it on the job. This may all sound negative, but what Spurgeon's did well was to give theological and Biblical input into my training. And that's what any Christian training programme will do – it won't train you for ministry, but it will make a contribution to your training.

I remain grateful to Spurgeon's. I'm grateful for the opportunity to study for four years, for the theological and Biblical input I did receive, for my interaction with lecturers and students, for stimulating a love of study and the reading of serious books and for underlining the importance of using commentaries when preparing to preach. I remember a few years ago listening to an elder preach on sanctification from a passage in Ephesians when in fact, the passage was all about justification. My conclusion was that he simply hadn't read a commentary. Spurgeon's had helped alert me to that danger.

Over the years, I know that Spurgeon's has developed a great deal, and probably most, if not all, of my criticisms here will have been addressed. However, I think that in the 1960s, the college was stuck in a bit of a rut, unaware or not even acknowledging what was happening at the grassroots level in the churches and not giving anywhere near enough attention to the realities of practical Christian leadership. However, something was happening in the student body itself, which was a warning of what was about to come.

Charismatic Rumblings

In the 1960s, many churches were being shaken, some blessed and some blighted, by what was commonly referred to as the charismatic movement. Pentecostal churches had been growing around the world since the beginning of the century, and what was now termed 'charismatic' certainly had similarities to Pentecostalism. But this movement was beginning to develop in more traditional churches. Anglican and Baptist churches were certainly being challenged by what was happening. Briefly, many individual Believers were claiming a fresh experience of the Holy Spirit, normally referred to as Baptism in the Spirit and with this came a renewed belief in speaking in tongues and all the spiritual gifts, such as prophecy, mentioned in the New Testament, as being relevant and available today. Perhaps what distinguished the charismatic from Pentecostalism as such was the lack of dogma regarding speaking in tongues being an absolute sign of Baptism in the Spirit.

This new life was spilling into Spurgeon's College, and a number of students claiming to have experienced this fresh baptism, or at least interested in what was happening, began to meet in a prayer group. I joined a few of these prayer meetings, but there were some 'Spirit-given' pictures shared, some of which I frankly felt uncomfortable with. In fairness, these were very early days in charismatic experience, and it is not surprising if there was some indiscipline and naivete reflected in what was accepted at the time. However, I was on a journey to test out what I could embrace in what was happening. I was very influenced by the teaching of Martyn Lloyd-Jones on the subject, something to which I will return.

The formation of these prayer meetings were soon picked up by the college faculty, who called a meeting of the staff and students. As I remember it, the position of the staff was sympathetic but not supportive. One of our lecturers came out with the statement, 'What we always have to remember is that the Holy Spirit is a gentleman.' That one sentence on its own was almost enough to send me charismatic! At the time, the outcome of this was the departure of one student as it was deemed that his theological views were probably not helpful in a Baptist College. After that, I think the prayer group somewhat fizzled out.

It was not helpful in the college to cut off discussion about what was now happening in some Baptist churches, which were becoming 'charismatic' and, therefore, an unwillingness to look at the issue in-depth and prepare us for what many of us would find on leaving the college.

Student Pastor

As students, we would often receive invitations to preach on a Sunday. Sometimes this was simply a personal invitation from a Baptist Church, and sometimes a church would write to the college and ask for a student preacher for a particular Sunday, in which case any of us might be offered the invitation. Needless to say, these were often small and struggling churches, though not always. I once preached in a large Baptist Church in Nottingham and then received an invitation for a second visit which felt quite heartwarming! What we really dreaded was being sent to address meetings of older ladies who met on midweek afternoons. This privilege was reserved for first-year students but became something of a challenge when Dr Beasley-Murray shared that as a student, he would try and be so interesting that the ladies stopped knitting!

What happened to the preaching fees was a somewhat archaic arrangement that I know got scrapped once I had left college. All those who had preached on a Sunday had to hand in their fee to a central pool. This was then added together and dispersed equally among the students but only according to year. So if you were in year one, you might all receive two shillings (in old money) but four shillings, six shillings and eight shillings in the other years. The basic unit, such as two shillings, was announced every week, usually to loud shouts of 'not enough.' There was always a holding back of money in the Christmas term so that on the last week, there would be a bumper amount announced. I seem to remember that wasn't ever considered enough, either!

In my second year, I took on a Student Pastorate, meaning that every other week I was at the same church. Mine was in a village called Sindlesham near Reading. The small congregation accepted me warmly as I preached twice every other Sunday, which was quite demanding as I had to prepare these two new messages in the midst of a busy college life. It was probably even more demanding on my listeners. Sue often came with me, and we were discreetly accommodated on a Saturday night in separate homes at either end of the village. I can't even remember the church having a toilet facility, but we were definitely in and out in the hour, so it probably wasn't necessary! Unlike today when services are longer or bladders weaker?

Marriage

Some students were accepted into Spurgeon's having already married, but for others who were falling in love while studying there, when one could marry was sometimes quite a battle with the Principal. The rule was that you were not allowed to marry until the summer vacation before the final year, and this is one reason for my long engagement with Sue. One student in my year really did fight it out with the Principal and managed to get married one year earlier than had previously been allowed. This, though, set a precedent so that by the year after I left Spurgeon's, the marriage rule was dropped altogether. Discussing it with one of the Tutors on a visit back to the college, he dryly remarked, 'If the door is about to be knocked down, there is an argument for opening it.'

Student flats tended to be passed on year to year by the older married students who graduated, and so after our wedding in 1968 and then a honeymoon in Scotland, when we toured around in an old Morris Minor with no heater, we found ourselves in one of these for the first year of our marriage. It was a large top-floor flat in an old house near the college – a house which was later bequeathed to the college by the owner. So for my final year, I would walk to the college each day. Sue would catch a train to central London, where she worked on a magazine as an assistant to Mary Berry – something you can find referred to in Mary Berry's autobiography. One advantage of Sue's work is that she would sometimes arrive home with a recipe that she had been testing that day. So there were quite a few exotic meals for a Baptist student.

Reunions

Every year Spurgeon's holds a College Conference and invites back all previous students at the college. I attended these while at college and then probably just a couple more in the years immediately after I left. The charismatic movement was very much in discussion on those Conference occasions. Some Baptist Pastors were embracing what was happening, and some definitely were not.

During one open discussion, a brother rose to his feet, stating that the previous Sunday, he'd attended as a visitor another Baptist Church where people were raising their hands in worship, which, he complained, completely blocked his view of the front of the building! The discussion tended to be more emotive than rational. On another occasion, a very well-known Baptist preacher and Keswick speaker were asked to address the subject of worship. This was obviously done with one eye on what was happening in those Baptist churches that had 'gone charismatic.' He spoke for a full hour and spent his entire time talking about preaching. That had to say something about a rather narrow view of worship that was held by some Baptist ministers at that time.

Over the next fifty years, our college year (like many others) held a series of reunions where those of us who'd studied together for four years met up to share our experiences. We held four of these, of which I attended three, and the last one was dubbed 'the ultimate reunion' and held fifty years after we had graduated. Our numbers dropped over the years; at that last one, just six of us were present. By then, I think six had died, and another six were too frail or simply not wanting to attend. On previous occasions, the conversation had been mainly some casual sharing of our previous few years, but I suggested at this last one that it might be good if three of us could give short papers. I was, as I hoped, asked to speak on ministry outside of the Baptist denomination. I was very careful to honour my Baptist background and in no way wanted to appear superior about belonging to a different family of churches, but I did give reasons why I didn't remain a Baptist pastor, and I talked about some of the positives that I felt I'd experienced since being involved with NewFrontiers while noting that some things we tried to do differently didn't always work. For example, I mentioned Christmas, which, in the early days of NewFrontiers, we'd try to invest with a much more charismatic flavour rather than the typical carol service. However, over the course of time, we'd swung back to a more traditional approach to Christmas and found this far more successful in seeing visitors join us. One of the group observed to me afterwards that it was good to hear that the NewFrontiers churches had now reverted to a Baptist style of church life – which is hardly what I was saying and shows the human tendency to hear only what you want to hear.

As I look back, I think up to six of my year retired as Baptist pastors; perhaps 3 of us found our way into different full-time ministries, and the rest left the ministry for other jobs. Some should never have come to the college in the first place, a point I will pick up when I write about my years teaching at Moorlands Bible College.

I walked out of Spurgeon's College after our ultimate reunion, thinking I shall never enter this building again, and felt rather sad about it; there were a lot of good memories connected with my time there.

Graduation

Before I graduated from the college in 1969, fifty years before that final reunion, I wrote to the recently retired Dr Martyn Lloyd-Jones to ask for some advice on thinking through Baptism in the Spirit. I knew he didn't hold the then-traditional evangelical view on the subject, and you can see this by reading through his sermons on Romans 8 in his thirteen-volume series of expositions on Paul's great epistle. I explained I was about to become a Baptist Pastor and asked for his help. He wrote back a gracious handwritten letter saying he wished he could see me to talk to, but his crowded diary made it impossible. However, he did recommend some books, particularly works by R A Torrey on the Holy Spirit. I wasn't really approaching the subject from the current charismatic angle at the time, but more from a Reformed perspective. But I was certainly thinking and praying. This was to become highly significant in my first Pastorate.

Chapter 3

Southampton

If a Baptist Pastor believed it was time to move on to a new church, he would usually contact his Area Superintendent – a kind of Free Church Bishop – who would give advice and would be able to tell him of churches that were looking for a new Minister so that introductions could then be made. In the case of college students, these Area Superintendents would know of churches that were willing to have a candidate straight from college and would make those known to the college. Through this process, the name of Bitterne Park Baptist Church in Southampton was mentioned to me, and introductions were made. The usual routine was a meeting with the church deacons and a so-called 'preach with a view' when the potential candidate would go once or twice to speak at the Sunday Services. If that went well, the deacons would recommend your name to the church, which would then vote on whether an invitation should be sent to you. You were always informed about the size of the vote, so if 70% voted in favour and 30% against, then you might have paused for thought. Really you were hoping for a 90-100% vote in favour, but there were always likely to be a few older people who felt you spoke too softly or too fast and so voted against it! I believe I received a 100% vote in favour, and so a few weeks after leaving college, we arrived in Southampton.

Bitterne Park is a suburb of the city not far from the centre. The Baptist Church building was long established, on a corner plot, with a fairly limited seating capacity and a rather utilitarian back hall. There were about 70 members. I began my ministry the same week as the first man walked on the moon. That small step was important for me, but it wasn't a great leap for mankind! We settled into our three-bedroom semi, which was owned by the church and had been redecorated for us by a couple of older men in the congregation. The workmanship wasn't great, but at least we had some say about what went on the walls. Another local Baptist Pastor told me that when he moved into his house, the wallpaper and paint had been chosen by the Sunday School children! You can imagine…. This was the same friend who had a Mrs Jelly as a church member, but his rather difficult mother-in-law, as he viewed her, didn't help his pastoral care when she rather, unfortunately, addressed her as Mrs Blancmange.

Mr Martin was the church secretary, his wife was the backup, and his sister-in-law (who also lived with them) was the church treasurer. This pointed to a degree of control by the one family, and the church was sometimes referred to as St Martins. However, they were nothing but helpful and supportive, though perhaps a little protective of the church they'd been part of for many years. Our first two years were good. I understood my role as preaching at two services on Sunday – taking care to keep the meetings to an hour - leading a mid-week Bible study, visiting church members and keeping the deacons on board. The worst bit was the monthly church members' meeting. This always had the potential to get tetchy. At one meeting, I proposed that we move the Sunday evening service in the summer months from 6.30 pm to 7 pm, whereupon one previously faithful church member publicly responded by saying he wouldn't come any more. I think my proposal failed, and it certainly got me thinking about that style of church government.

Sue has always been an outstanding pastor's wife, and she got stuck in with the routine of church life. One of our members was a formidable older lady called Miss George. Her role within the church was to lead the 'Sisterhood', which was a weekly gathering of other older ladies in the church for a devotional meeting supplemented by tea and cake. Bear in mind that Sue was only 24 at this point, but as the new pastor's wife, she was invited to a

Prayer Meeting about the Sisterhood. The nominal head of the Sisterhood was the President, a role often, but not necessarily filled by the pastor's wife. The vacancy had occurred due to the departure of the previous pastor and wife. Sue's duty to fill the role was made very clear when in the Prayer Meeting, Miss George prayed that the Lord would put it in Sue's heart to become President. Sue felt she could resist neither God or Miss George! When we left the church four years later, two young single ladies who had been lodging with us attended a Prayer Meeting in connection with the call of a new pastor. Miss George was passionate in prayer again: 'Lord give us a man, give us a man.' The two young ladies informed us that they had joined in with fervent amens as they echoed her cry, also asking that the Lord would give them a man.

A few years later, I heard that Miss George had received a diagnosis of terminal cancer, which she handled with total tranquillity. She died strong in faith.

So, during those first two years, we saw some steady growth, a few conversions, some baptisms and other Christians joining us. The building became fairly full both morning and evening, and the membership edged towards a hundred. I was responsible for leading every part of the Sunday Services except the notices, which were handled by Mr Martin, the highpoint of which was always the total for the collection the previous week: 'Last week's offering was nineteen pounds, seven shillings and sixpence.'

Then the charismatic time bomb detonated.

Painful Times

I can't remember the precise chronology of events, but these are some of the things that definitely happened.

The charismatic influence was more and more taking hold in local churches and was causing some very tense situations, as was the case in our church. A number of our members gave testimony to being baptised in the Holy Spirit. They felt this was having a profound influence on their lives and was something that should be fully accepted in our church life, where it would make a real difference to the congregation as a whole. This was not well received by many older members.

One of the stand-out memories of my life was an evening some of us visited Basingstoke Baptist Church, led at the time by Barney Coombs. The church was gaining a reputation for being strongly charismatic and for the major changes that were taking place in the life of the church. One week they ran a number of Praise evenings led by a group from America called: The New Creation Singers. Some of us decided to go. Among our group was a young couple who had recently joined us. Mike and Jane were clearly Christians, but Jane was overwhelmingly shy. This meant she had never been baptised as a Believer because she simply couldn't face up to being immersed in water in front of a crowd of people, let alone give public testimony. The meeting was lively, and the Band was great; the congregation was full of praise. Mike and Jane were in the row behind me, and in the middle of one of the songs, Jane suddenly fell flat out along the pew – something that didn't happen in Baptist churches! I was really quite frightened, especially as I was her pastor. I grabbed Barney Coombs, whom I knew slightly, pulled him out of the building and told him she was one of our church congregation; what was happening to her? He took it all very calmly and, in a sentence I'll never forget, said: 'Well, I don't know her; it's either an evil spirit or she's been baptised in the Spirit – you'll be able to tell when she comes round!' About 15 minutes later, she did come around and seemed to be all right; the meeting continued, and we returned home in different cars. It wasn't until the next day that I had a conversation with her. She told me she'd been on her feet singing and worshipping when suddenly she felt the Holy Spirit come on her with such force and power she was simply knocked off her feet (so much for the Holy Spirit always being a gentleman!). Jane was radically changed. She lost her shyness and shortly after she gave testimony to her faith and was baptised. Later on, Mike and Jane became part of the Southampton Community Church, where they made a huge contribution, and in contacts, we had in later years, I never saw them waver in their passion for their Christian faith.

Although influenced by the charismatic movement, it was through the teaching of Dr Martyn Lloyd-Jones that I became convinced there is a Baptism of the Spirit that is experiential and does not necessarily happen at the time of conversion. With so much happening around me, I became hungry for this and began to pray more urgently. I was praying in my study one morning when I had a very conscious experience of being filled as though liquid was being poured into me from the top of my head and down to the bottom of my feet, and at the same time, my arms went up in the air in a posture of worship and a stream of words poured out of my mouth which I knew was speaking in tongues, though I hadn't been seeking that as such. I was so overwhelmed that I didn't quite know what to do and wondered what my wife would think about this. So I recorded myself speaking in tongues and then later sat her down and played it to her, saying: 'What do you think about this?' We both realised that I had experienced a filling of the Spirit in a very distinct way. Sue had her own encounter with God in this way when a friend prayed with her sometime later.

As all of this was happening, a new pastor arrived to lead a Pentecostal Church on the other side of the city. He began to shake things up considerably, and very soon, Believers from other churches began to attend meetings in his church. He had a strong personality and a great passion for evangelism. Increasing numbers began to attract more people to see what was happening, and for those who were being drawn into the new charismatic movement but had a lack of support and even opposition in their own church, a lively Pentecostal Church seemed a good alternative.

I was completely out of my depth. I only had two years of experience as a pastor, no one with whom to talk, and my own experience of the Spirit, but at the same time, a group now in the church who having visited the Pentecostal Church seemed to want our Baptist Church to become a Pentecostal Church and fairly instantly as well. I fluffed around, but in all conscience, I didn't feel I should just try to turn our church into a Pentecostal Church. I realise now that maybe I could have got some more experienced leaders involved to help me, but at the time, it seemed that the only way for the tension to ease was through a split. So the charismatic group broke away to join the Pentecostal Church; it was extremely painful for a young, inexperienced pastor.

Meanwhile, something more specifically charismatic was beginning to surface at Southampton University under the gifted leadership of a student called Tony Moreton, who went on to plant and then lead what became known as the Southampton Community Church. Many years later, our second son, David, studied at Southampton University and joined the Community Church. Most of those who'd left us for the Pentecostal Church also, in time, transferred to the Community Church. There were multiple factors involved, but in those early days, where Pentecostals would have very much emphasised evangelism,

29

charismatics were emphasising worship and community, which was certainly an attraction to other Believers.

For the next year, my work was cut out trying to settle the church down after a split and also to rebuild, knowing that at the same time, I was leaning towards what was now happening in churches that were more sympathetic to this new move of the Spirit. I felt disillusioned with how things were working out, and I applied for and was offered a teaching job at a nearby Boy's Grammar School. The deacons agreed to me taking the job, so for the rest of my time in Southampton, I taught Religious Studies in a School while continuing to lead the church in Bitterne Park. In this rather confusing period of my life, I began to feel a growing conviction that I was really meant to be a pastor rather than a school teacher, but working in a school was, in many ways, a positive and challenging experience.

People have sometimes asked me how I changed after being baptised in the Spirit. I believe I changed in a number of ways, but primarily, it was theological. In all that had happened, I realised that I had no clear doctrine of the church. Extraordinary as this may sound today, in my first couple of years as a Baptist Pastor, I didn't have a clue as to what it meant for the church to be the Body of Christ. I knew the term was in the Bible, of course, but I assumed it was a mystical description of the church. In Spurgeon's, we'd had no real teaching on the church at all, and I had simply absorbed and implemented the way that Baptist Churches seemed to be organised. Following this new experience of the Spirit, I began to see something of what the church was meant to be and expressed in a way I'd never seen before. For me, this was a huge positive from being baptised in the Spirit.

Moving On

I knew it was time for me to start again in another church, but a few other things are worth mentioning at this point. This was my first experience of broken relationships in a local church. Some of those who left during this time were those whom I had come most to rely on. They welcomed me warmly when I came and were initially extremely supportive and enthusiastic about my ministry. I suppose I took that support as an indication of loyalty and friendship. It was emotionally extremely difficult when I obviously failed to give them what they wanted, and they left. If you are a pastor, whatever people say, you feel like a personal failure when people leave. So often, those who go will tell you that it's not personal, but it always feels as though it is. One thing you cannot avoid in leading a church is that people leave you, and sometimes it is those who had seemed to be most supportive. Again and again, I've heard leaders say that the most painful part of being in Christian ministry is broken relationships. It's something you have to learn to deal with, but at the same time, I do think there is too much of it.

While in Southampton, I became very unimpressed by the function of a Baptist diaconate. Men and women were voted into that role by the church members. I think there was too much of the idea around that they were having there to keep a check on the minister! This was underlined to me when I asked one of my deacons, who was recently retired from work but very practical with his hands, if he could take responsibility for keeping a check on the material condition of the buildings and let us know when things should be attended to. He refused, and though he apologised later, he never fulfilled the role. I couldn't help but think, what are any of the deacons for? All that changed later when I came to appreciate the role of elders.

I made a very bad mistake while we were there about the house that we lived in. It was the official Church Manse, owned by the church and made available for whoever was the pastor at the time. I knew of Baptist Pastors who'd died young, and the widow eventually had to leave the Manse without anywhere satisfactory to go. To protect Sue from that possibility, I was determined we should try to buy our own house. I asked the deacons if we could buy the Manse as we had the promise of some financial help from Sue's mother. They agreed with the condition that they had the first choice on re-buying the property if we ever sold it. At that point, houses were generally undervalued, so we made our purchase at the current market value. This was very reasonable, so we went ahead and had an easy move into our own property! Shortly after, for the first time, property prices began to boom in a way that has continued on and off to this day. By modern standards, the price was still very cheap, but our house went up quite considerably in value. So when we were leaving, the deacons made it pretty clear that they didn't expect to pay the new market price for the property that they'd allowed us to buy. In the end, I felt a compromise was the best way through, and we halved the increased value. I learned a lesson that a pastor should never mix his finances with the church's finances.

Before leaving Southampton, I was asked if I would give a series of lectures at Moorlands Bible College near Bournemouth. Though I did not know it at the time, this was to be significant for what happened some years later.

But for now, we were moving to Kent.

Chapter 4

Whitstable

Near the end of 1973, we moved to Whitstable in Kent. We were now a family of four, our two sons, Matthew and David, having been born in Southampton General Hospital before we moved. David was very nearly born on the way to the hospital. Sue woke me early one morning, saying the baby was on the way, and I went into the bathroom for a leisurely wash and shave. Things turned a lot more urgent as Sue stood in the bathroom doorway saying. 'We've got to go *now.*' I rushed her into the car and drove at high speed through mostly empty streets due to the time of day, but inwardly panicked all the way that the car was running on empty. I'd meant to fill up with petrol the day before, and now I was desperately wishing that I had. But we made it to the hospital door, and within minutes our second son was born.

We arrived at our next Baptist Church through the conventional route of contacting the Area Superintendent. I'd chatted with him about our difficulties in Southampton and my conviction that I shouldn't continue in teaching but should move on to lead another church. He introduced us to Swalecliffe Free Church (Baptist). Swalecliffe is at the Eastern end of the small town of Whitstable in North Kent. When the area was developed, it was agreed that there should be one Free or non-conformist church to serve it, but the decision was made to link it to the Baptist Union, which is how it came to have its title. There was often a reference to the church being Baptist in brackets, which was in a way to prove prophetic. When I received the invitation to become the minister of the church, both Sue and I felt it was right to accept. I'd been to the church a couple of times and met with the deacons. It was clear that a group of the younger deacons were on the same journey as we were spiritually. They'd been baptised

33

in the Spirit and were looking for a more radical expression of church life. I could tell that, like us, they really wanted to work out in practise what it meant for the church to be the Body of Christ.

We began what was a real adventure lasting around ten years. During that time, the church membership grew from 140 to about 210, and there was considerable growth in church attendance.

Swalecliffe itself is a small residential area but not far from the University of Kent. While we were there, students from the University discovered our church and began to attend in quite reasonable numbers. Over the years, a number were baptised as Believers. But we were also situated just 3 miles away from a Christian Conference Centre.

Herne Bay Court

The Court was quite well known among evangelical churches as an excellent centre for Conferences and church weekends. It could accommodate about 200 and had good facilities. The lounge, where meetings were generally held, was a bit cramped, but there was an excellent dining room, an outdoor swimming pool, some good sports facilities and plenty of outside space. Over the years, the majority of the staff who ran the Court decided to come to our church. But in terms of swelling the numbers in our congregation, the real boost came in the summer holidays when Herne Bay Court functioned as a Christian holiday centre. Holiday makers were encouraged to attend a local church on Sundays as there were no meetings held at the centre itself. Many of them found their way to us, especially as our reputation as a church experiencing some degree of charismatic renewal began to circulate. This reputation would also have kept some holiday makers away from us! Because we were attracting students, holiday makers, Herne Bay Court staff and increasingly visitors from nearby Canterbury, our building was sometimes filled to the extent that we had to run an overflow meeting in the church lounge.

After we left the area, Herne Bay Court, which must have incurred huge upkeep costs, could no longer pay its way and was sold off to provide land for a new housing development. I do wonder if their rather rigid rules also contributed to their demise. During the summer period, though the holidays were obviously popular, there was a management style which was probably off-putting for many people. Most summers I was invited to be the Speaker for one of the holiday weeks. This was great; our young sons thoroughly enjoyed the facilities, and it was a free holiday week for the family. However, it was all a bit heavy. Every morning we were woken up by a burst of heavenly music at about 7 or 7.30, and this was followed by the verse for the day, often being read as holiday makers in dressing gowns gathered at various tea points in the corridors to collect an early morning 'cuppa.' Breakfast was eaten by everyone at the same time, but you couldn't leave before the visiting Speaker (me) had delivered a 10-minute thought-for-the-day. Then, and remember this was a holiday, there was a daily evening meeting. Of course, no-one was forced to attend, but most people did, and you'd be 'missed' if you weren't there. So Monday to Friday, I'd give a 20-30 minute Bible exposition.

I'd often heard that it was best to avoid the 'Irish week.' But one summer, I landed it. Every year a group of Irish Brethren would meet up together at Herne Bay. It was different! There were quite a few young men in the group, which was good, but they were a tough audience to preach to. Each evening I would speak without a flicker of response from anyone. Now that may not surprise you, but the whole hour felt incredibly solemn and uptight. What followed the meeting was rather startling as some of the congregation went berserk. Pillows were thrown out of windows, water was splattered around, and the young men went shouting up and down the corridors; it was like a mini-riot. They might not have found the meeting too much fun, but they certainly let off steam afterwards.

Another year I was the Speaker at the Christmas House Party. This was also run as a holiday week. I decided to do a series of talks on The Apostle's Creed. In keeping with the Herne Bay Court style, this meant that I was asked to give one of the talks in the middle of the Christmas Day evening party. Unfortunately, I had just reached the phrase, 'he descended into hell.' It simply wasn't the best talk for the moment!

This holiday was also the occasion when my wife's early infatuation with my knees, which I mentioned in chapter 1, bore fruit. We played some awful party games. One of these required a team of men to roll up their trousers above their knees. Then the wives were blindfolded, the husbands were moved to random chairs, and the ladies had to go along the row feeling the men's knees. Who could tell which was their husband? All the other women went right along the row, had a think and made their choice. Some of them were right, and some were wrong. Sue went down the row, but as soon as she touched my knees, she declared, 'that's my husband.' She was the outright winner!

A major cause of unsanctified thoughts was the swimming pool. This was very popular with a good seating area around it, and a lot of the holiday was enjoyed there, except on a Sunday. There was an absolute rule that the pool was closed on Sunday, and there was to be no swimming. This was a fascinating example of what legalism does. I can remember hot Sunday afternoons with everyone sitting round the pool, longing to be in the pool, with everybody in the pool in their mind but not in their body.

Inevitably, a teenager would sit on the edge of the pool and put their feet in. It wasn't long before there were a lot of teenage feet being dangled in the pool. Then a boy would flick some water at a girl sitting nearby, and so it went on. Everyone knew it would have been far better for the pool to be open rather than causing a great deal of rule-bending and frustration.

The Dales

Slowly our church worship began to change. For a time, this only happened at the evening service. We began to introduce other instruments, including drums, alongside the electronic organ. We started to sing new songs that weren't in the Baptist hymn book. The evening service took on a much freer and more open style of worship. Our sense of community kept growing. On Sunday, we stayed on to eat lunch together. A number of members moved to the area nearer to the church building to identify more strongly with the community feel. We had church holidays together. We started an early morning prayer meeting on Sundays, and we had tongues and interpretation in that setting. For a time, the same brother was bringing a tongue every week, which I eventually limited in a way that was perhaps a bit heavy-handed. An increasingly charismatic atmosphere was growing along with our motivation to discover how to be a more obvious Christian community.

In 1978 a group of us went to the Dales Bible Week, held near Harrogate. Over the years, I've spoken to many individuals who were at that particular Bible week and remembered it well. It was hosted by Bryn Jones, one of the best-known charismatic leaders at that time, and it was huge. It was also wet; the rain poured down most of the week. None of us had ever before been in a meeting of thousands of people with full-on charismatic worship. It was both slightly scary and electrifying. The guest speaker for the week was Bob Mumford, an American preacher. He spoke each evening on the theme of the Kingdom of God, and one of his messages took a full ninety minutes!

With the changes that were taking place in our church, I intuitively knew that there was something missing. Towards the end of the week, Bob Mumford spoke on spiritual authority. I was deeply impacted; I came out of that meeting and, standing in the drizzle, said to Sue, 'that's it - it's the issue of spiritual authority.' At that moment, I knew I was no longer a Baptist Pastor.

I am certainly not hostile towards the Baptist denomination. There are many excellent Baptist Churches, and I still describe myself as 'baptistic' because I am firmly convinced of the rightness of a Believer's Baptism and the priesthood of all Believers, which are particular Baptist emphases. However, I was uncomfortable with how these beliefs were worked out. Both Baptist Churches I pastored were 'open membership' churches, meaning you could become a member without being baptised as a Believer if you didn't want to be. I thought that was odd. I was increasingly uncomfortable with leading a church which was publicly signed as Baptist. Why display a church title which underlines a point of theological disagreement with other churches? A name like Trinity Church also indicates doctrinal belief, but one that is agreed by all true churches. Moreover, the priesthood of all Believers was really only worked out by the fact that all the church members could turn up at the regular church meetings, propose actions that the pastor and deacons had not even discussed and participate in a vote on really quite trivial issues. So often, these meetings were unproductive and had a distinctly negative feel. I remember a time that we asked the church to vote on whether we could turn the church seating around to give a better feel of a community as we worshipped together. But what about the pulpit, someone asked; what would we do with it? Much debate followed on this, and one member proposed that we fix wheels to the pulpit so we could move it easily to wherever we felt we needed it in the building! Bob Mumford's message liberated me. Surely the right way forward was to recognise the men God was raising up to lead the church (the Bible calls them elders), and they would take the church forward unhindered by votes and church meetings.

Soon we recognised we had four elders who made up the leadership team together with me, and 'Baptist' was now definitely in brackets. But that's when our troubles began.

Terry Virgo

There was a young man in our fellowship who went to London to train as a nurse. While he was there, he attended a church that Terry Virgo was involved with. He gave us some enthusiastic feedback on how the church was flourishing with Terry's input. One summer, Ian, this church's lead elder, came on holiday to our area. He drove past our church building and, for no particular reason, decided he'd visit us on Sunday. While he was sitting in the meeting the next day, it suddenly dawned on him that this was where the student nurse attending his church must have come from. After the Service was over, he came to speak to me, and very soon, we were into a long conversation about the help he and his church had received from Terry Virgo's ministry.

Some three months later, Ian rang me late on a Friday evening. He apologised for leaving it to the last moment but said I'd be very welcome to attend a leader's meeting the next morning at Haywards Heath in Sussex. Terry Virgo would be speaking. Not only was this a very late invitation, but the next morning I was supposed to be gathering our elders at home for one of our regular meetings. There was no way I could disappear to Sussex at about 7.30 am.

After a very restless night, I got up early, told Sue to apologise to the elders and asked them to get on with things without me. I felt I had to go to listen to Terry Virgo. That decision changed the course of my life, and I'm forever grateful for it. I have no memory of anything that Terry said that morning, but I came away thinking; he was articulating the vision I share for what a local church can be.

I was really excited by what Terry had taught and said to the Elders that they must come with me to the next leader's day. A few meetings later, we'd heard enough to agree as elders that we needed some input, but we were nervous about asking Terry to visit us. We felt that the church might be a bit overwhelmed by Terry's ministry, but we had a cunning plan.

There was an older pastor serving on Terry's team who was based with him at Clarendon Church in Brighton. Henry Tyler had been a Baptist Minister for many years, and even better, we had members in our church who had previously belonged to one of the churches that Henry had led. We saw this as a good way to introduce our church to the kind of message that Terry was teaching without asking Terry himself. Something of a comic event followed. At the next leader's gathering, we approached Henry as a group, explained some of our church life and asked if he would come to us for a Sunday. 'I'd love to,' said Henry, 'but I'm just about to go into hospital for an ear operation, but I know Terry would want to come.' Then raising his voice, he shouted across the room to Terry Virgo, 'Hey, Terry, these guys would like you to come and preach at their church.' That is how we landed a two-Sunday visit from Terry Virgo!

Terry seemed to warm to us. We chatted with him as a team of elders and agreed to pursue a friendship with him. The Downs

Bible Weeks in Sussex, led by Terry, had now started, and we took a good number from the church to those.

However, there was a sense of increasing tension in the church, and strong differences of opinion surfaced. On the one hand, there was a group who wanted us to go fully into what Terry was then pioneering with a new church movement, but there were others who definitely wanted to hold to our Baptist roots and structures. One of the issues that was becoming clearer at this time was that Terry and, indeed, other influential leaders weren't just proposing a kind of charismatic dimension to church life but the complete renewal of church life. The word most often used at that time was 'Restoration,' as the vision was of a restoration to New Testament Church life. It was also a time when some were leaving traditional churches and meeting in homes (referred to as the House Church movement). Over the years, many of these groups became far too large to meet in a house and had to move to other buildings. Initially, there was some resistance to buying buildings as the feeling was that money should be put into ministry rather than property. I sometimes smile to myself when I think back to a time when these then-new churches would have owned hardly any property, whereas today, the collective value of NewFrontiers church buildings alone would undoubtedly be in the hundreds of millions.

The church was growing, we were becoming more charismatic, and we had recognised elders, but there was still a very tense atmosphere. I'm sure that some of our members felt nothing of this, but I could sense we were heading for a split. I remember months of going into the evening meeting, both excited and yet scared. Suppose someone spoke in a tongue, and no one interpreted it. I was close to thinking the ground might open up and swallow us! Over the years, I've spoken to a number of men who were leaders at that time and went though a very similar experience.

Around this time, Moorlands Bible College contacted me. They remembered that I had done some lecturing a few years earlier when we lived in Southampton, and they would like to interview me for the post of New Testament Lecturer. The interview went well, and they invited me to take the role. After an initial refusal on my part, they renewed the invitation, and some months later, I accepted.

I look back on that time with mixed feelings. I think the tension was beginning to burn me out. Rightly or wrongly, because I'd been there nearly ten years, I believed that the church trusted me and was holding together around me. But in my heart, I wanted to move on and embrace wholeheartedly what Terry Virgo was teaching, but I knew if we did that, the church would split. After working so hard for so many years to build a strong sense of community, I didn't have the conviction that I should precipitate a division. In a way, I took the easy option and left. But I also left the problem to someone else. The church called a new minister who held similar convictions to mine, but he hadn't been there long enough to build up the confidence of the congregation, so the church did split. I'm not proud of what happened. Sue and I have talked a number of times over the years about whether we should have stayed and seen it through. In many respects, they were very exciting years. We touched a dimension of community in church life that we've never enjoyed in the same way since. But it was fragile, being somewhat inward-looking, and church splits can cause a lot of pain. I think there were some who were very sorry to see us go, but probably others who felt we left something of a mess behind us. A lot was changing in church life at that time; there were splits in many other churches and new churches being formed. Out of it all, new church movements arose. In time the group of churches that Terry was leading came to be called NewFrontiers. That became the family of Churches we were to spend our following years with, but it didn't happen immediately.

Chapter 5

Moorlands Bible College

As soon as we arrived at Moorlands, we were thinking about leaving again. Soon after we moved into our new house, Sue was praying whilst working in the garden, and she asked God how long we'd be there. Her testimony is that she heard an audible voice:'Three years.' And so it proved to be.

The College Campus is about 3 miles north of the Bournemouth conurbation, which comprises three connected towns, Bournemouth, Christchurch and Poole, with a combined population of about 400,000. Our house was in Christchurch, and it was an easy drive, or occasionally a cycle ride, to the college.

Moorlands was originally established as a training college for members of Brethren Assemblies who felt called to missionary work, but over time moved its premises and its affiliations to become an independent evangelical training college. There have been several building programs over the years, and the college now has very good facilities on large grounds. I joined the staff when Dr Derek Copley was the Principal. He had a scientific background but had previously planted a church in the Manchester area. He was a gracious but reserved man. He gave good leadership to the college, but I never felt I really got to know him very well.

The atmosphere was less academic than it had been at Spurgeon's. The student group was quite young, with a few older persons and married couples. I was to have an ongoing link with 3 of the older students. Courses lasted 2 to 3 years, and there was a diploma awarded for completion of studies, though later, they developed degree courses at the college. I was mainly involved in teaching the New Testament but also lectured in Theology and tutored the first two years in New Testament Greek; another lecturer doing more advanced studies in Greek if students stayed on for a third year. Greek was the least popular of the subjects that were taught. It involves a lot of memory work to learn the Greek used in the Bible as it is not the same as modern Greek, which is spoken today, so there is no conversational element to it. I think a lot of students felt frustrated with the effort involved in learning verb tables and vocabulary. From Spurgeon's, I had a good grasp of the language, which I kept going to some degree when I was a pastor, but inevitably I was a bit rusty. It wouldn't have been too hard to keep ahead of the groups I was teaching had it not been for one young woman who was joining the Wycliffe Bible Translators. She was clearly gifted at languages and had no trouble learning Greek. Streaks ahead of the rest of the class; she certainly kept me on my toes! It was also a time when creative writing and expression were the current trendy way of teaching English, and very little attention had been given to grammar. Greek requires you to know about verbs, adjectives, prepositions etc. Most of the students simply didn't have a clue; they hadn't been taught English in that way. There was even a student who had previously been an English teacher in a school who didn't really understand what a verb was! However, we had a handful of Dutch students who had been taught English grammar in their school system, and they had a big advantage over the other students. Anyway, we battled on, though the Bible's exhortations about not grumbling didn't seem to be applied too well when learning New Testament Greek!

Altogether there was a much more informal environment than I had known at Spurgeon's. Now fourteen years on from my graduation, this reflected the fact that there was more informality in society generally. Students and Tutors were all on first-name terms, and during the lunch breaks, some of us on staff played sports with the students. We also had a system of Tutor groups which meant that every lecturer was pastorally responsible for about a dozen students, and we met together as a group one afternoon every week. We could use our time to talk or pray together or for some social activity. I remember, one afternoon, dragging the group down to a museum in Bournemouth, where they were collectively unimpressed. This may be why having returned to live in the area in retirement, it took my wife twelve years to get me back to the same museum.

One of the Tutor group, Tony Priscott, was an ex-professional football player for Bournemouth and a few years older than me. We struck up a good friendship, and sometime later, I worked with him to plant a church in Ringwood, a few miles outside of Bournemouth. Another older couple was already assistant leaders of a church in Hampshire, which later helped me to develop a very strong link there, and in time, that church also joined the NewFrontiers family of churches.

We soon discovered that my being a lecturer in a Bible College was tough for us financially. We were now responsible for paying a mortgage rather than living in a Manse provided by the church. Because of the house purchase back in our Southampton days, and the subsequent purchase of another house that we had bought in Kent and rented out before selling, we had enough money for a deposit, but the mortgage payments certainly ate into my salary. Four of us on staff had begun as new Tutors at the same time, and through private conversations, we discovered that all of us were really struggling financially. One of the four had previously been a missionary in South America and fulfilled that role of 'living by faith.' In other words, he had no guaranteed income, but he had to pray for his support. His testimony was that he'd been better off living by faith than by receiving a guaranteed salary! As a group, we approached the Principal and explained our situation. We were all interviewed by the College Trustees, and the happy outcome was a pay rise.

However, we still needed to top up our income, and so for the first time since our two sons had been born, Sue returned to work for a year, cooking lunch for the children at a small private school and then for the rest of our time we lived there she worked, part-time, in a coffee shop that was linked to our church.

Church Life

The obvious church for us to join was Christchurch Baptist. We lived near where they met, and they also had a link with Terry Virgo. I was asked to join the leadership team, and I remained on it for the years that we were there. Mick Frisby was the leader of the church, and he asked me to preach quite regularly, and we worked well together. Besides preaching in other local churches, I was also asked to become Moderator of Alder Road Baptist Church in Poole. At this time, I was still an accredited Baptist Minister. When Baptist Churches were without a lead Pastor, as Alder Road was then, for their pastor had just moved to lead a church in America, another Baptist Pastor was often asked if he could come in and help the church until a new minister was appointed. He was known as the Moderator. Over the next three years, I preached there quite often, met with the deacons, chaired the church meetings (oh joy!) and generally tried to assist the church in finding a new leader. At the time I was leaving the area three years later, a new pastor was inducted to lead the church. Little did I know then how significant my involvement with Alder Road would prove to be for our family. Of which, more later.

Meanwhile, at Christchurch Baptist, there was almost a rerun of our time at Swalecliffe Free Church. The church enjoyed a very open style of worship, and there was talk about appointing elders, although they hadn't yet taken that step. Terry Virgo visited and talked with the leaders, we attended the Downs Bible Weeks, and Mick was determined to make a full link with Terry's ministry and, therefore, for the church to cease to be Baptist. At this point, the Baptist Union became involved. So we not only had a visit from Terry but from Baptist Union officials as well! In fairness to the Baptist Union, there was a strong feeling among those officials that it was right to uphold the Trust Deeds of the church, and that required not only that we practised Believers' Baptism, which of course we were doing, but for us to operate with congregational government, meaning, as at Swalecliffe: that all the church members were entitled to vote on all issues in connection with the church. At that time, the Baptist Union was observing a number of their churches wanting to move away from that style of government towards elders who had the responsibility to lead and make decisions. It was a period when things were quite messy. Some churches changed their style of government and just kept quiet about it; some possibly fudged things a bit, and others, like ourselves, tried to debate it with the Baptist Union from a place of Biblical conviction. I heard of one church (though I'm not sure whether it was Baptist) that voted to stop voting! Those of us who were caught up in the changes taking place were often engaged in quite intense discussions with church members and other leaders about the nature of spiritual authority. I found when I finally left the Baptist denomination altogether that this issue hardly got mentioned. In our NewFrontiers churches, the congregation happily accepted that the elders led the church, and that was fine; no one was bothered about voting.

However, at Christchurch, our convictions brought us to a point where the Baptist Union asked us to leave the building. We weren't unique in this, but over the years, the Baptist Union has definitely softened their position and requests to vacate Baptist premises now seem to have stopped altogether. But we had to leave and decided to rent a hall in a nearby Holiday Camp on

Sunday mornings. Mick hoped that we would carry the whole church with us. So the plan was to close the Baptist building one Sunday, hand the keys to the Baptist Union and begin worshipping as New Covenant Church the same day. But when the day came, a minority decided to stay at the Baptist Church and continue as a local Baptist congregation, and that church has continued to thrive. At the same time, we had, in effect, planted a new church. Some years later, Citygate Church Bournemouth was planted out from the Christchurch congregation. Citygate now has a large membership and a multimillion-pound modern church building.

Invitation

During our first two years at Christchurch, with me teaching at the college and our involvement with events that took place in the church, Terry Virgo kept in touch with us and suggested that I should consider not spending too many years as a Bible College lecturer. I was, therefore, not totally surprised when he asked us to move down to Brighton and join the full-time team of Clarendon Church that he was leading and which was seeing quite rapid growth. I believed it was right to give a full year's notice to the college and not back out halfway through an academic year. My resignation was accepted, the college had a decent amount of time to find a replacement, and we moved to Brighton the following August, exactly three years after we had moved to Christchurch.

I've been grateful for every different part of my life, and that is certainly true of being a college lecturer. I believe my time at Moorlands helped me to think through my faith and Biblical convictions more fully. When you preach a sermon, one or two people may ask you a question afterwards. In a College environment, the questioning is relentless. I constantly had to justify my exegesis of the New Testament, and I couldn't skip over difficult issues. That was really helpful. I remember one very well-known Bible teacher who seemed to be offended and hurt if people questioned his interpretations or explanations, and another who didn't want to be challenged on anything he said and tried to prevent any questions from even being asked. I learned while teaching in college that my hearers really wanted to be convinced by the teaching they were given. It wasn't a matter of challenging me personally but of seeking to be satisfied that what I was saying was something they could accept. I've always welcomed questions when I've been teaching leadership groups, even if there have been individuals who didn't agree with all the answers!

Training

Over the years, I've been through a training program at Spurgeon's, taught at a Bible College and then been very involved in theological teaching and training in NewFrontiers. Not surprisingly, I've formed a few convictions about training Christian leaders. Crucially, those who are truly leaders are those who should be trained. I've already mentioned that there were some students at Spurgeon's who should never have been there, and that was also true at Moorlands. There is a danger that because of financial pressures, colleges need students as much as students need the colleges. The cost of maintaining buildings and paying staff wages in a college is huge, and students bring money into the college. There is a pressure, therefore, to allow in as many as possible; it helps pay the bills! At Moorlands, I began to see there were two matters that needed to be clear when interviewing candidates. One was, what leadership were they currently involved in? If none, why? The other was what would they do when they graduated? The latter issue was much easier at Spurgeon's because there was an almost guaranteed route into the Baptist ministry. Even so, when I was at Spurgeon's, you could tell there were some guys there who were never going to survive in ministry; they were just too awkward. When it came to it, there were plenty of gifted guys that fell out of leadership for a variety of reasons, but at least they showed initial promise. In a Bible College, the situation was even more pronounced. We had students come to Moorlands whose ambition was to get into some form of full-time Christian ministry. Some did and got invited to lead a church or joined up with a missionary organisation. But there were those who made a real sacrifice to be there, even selling up a house to pay the fees, but found that when they graduated from college, the Christian world wasn't waiting to employ them. For some, this proved quite devastating. I recognised this shortly after going on staff and tried to push for an agreement that we took real care to enquire whether a student had a realistic route into some job or ministry when they graduated. If not, then the time and expense of being at college probably weren't appropriate.

NewFrontiers training programs have always been part-time, although we have given the opportunity to those planning to go to University or who have just graduated to volunteer with a church for a year in a program that also provides theological input. This has never been with the expectation that it will lead to full-time ministry. Today, many young people take a 'gap year', and in our churches, there have been a number like this who have decided to give such a year to serving in a local church.

With our part-time courses, our aim has always been to input those who are already involved in leadership at some level in their church. Because it is a part-time study, the costs are comparatively low. We use properties that churches already own, and the teaching is given almost always by those who are already full-time leaders paid by their local churches. I was more than interested, therefore, when the Principal of Spurgeon's College talked about their financial challenges when I attended our Ultimate Reunion. Clearly, the cost of the premises was beginning to look overwhelming, and he was making some radical proposals to address that. He passed the comment that it would be vastly cheaper simply to rent rooms in a Best Western Hotel from time to time and give lectures there. I thought, well, that's essentially what we were doing, though we might use the premises of our church in Norwich, for example, rather than the Best Western! Obviously, colleges do have some advantages, not least a well-resourced library, though with what is now available to view on the Web, it makes even that less of an advantage than would have been the case in the past. Also, a full-time course taken in a college makes it much easier in terms of supervision of students, as everyone is immediately on hand. But if men and women are serious about the benefits that a training course gives, then it is up to them to do the work necessary even if constant supervision is not available.

I am grateful that in NewFrontiers, we have those who've specialised in particular subjects, such as Church history or Islamic studies, and taken higher degrees, but then opportunities to gain those degrees and doctorates exist in our Universities.

My brief ministry as a Bible College lecturer was now over. The story now moves to what I always think of as the main ministry of my life in Brighton.

Chapter 6

Clarendon Church

When we arrived in Brighton, or 'Hove actually' (it was a long-standing joke that those living in Hove always distanced themselves from Brighton with this phrase), Clarendon Church had existed for about seven years. Two Pastors, Henry Tyler from a Baptist background and Dave Fellingham, who'd been on staff at an Anglican Church, had come together with a small group of people to form the Brighton and Hove Christian Fellowship, which initially met in a school hall. They contacted Terry Virgo, who was then leading a church in Seaford, a few miles along the coast from Brighton, and asked for his help. Terry had grown up in Brighton and believed that God would one day take him back there. This seemed the right time, so Terry moved and took the lead of the new church. It grew quickly, and as Terry, Dave, and Henry prayed for a new meeting venue, they were offered a church building in Hove, along with its small congregation, known as The Clarendon Mission. The name was changed to Clarendon Church, and this became the home of the young church congregation.

By the time I arrived, there had been considerable growth, which meant that the church had needed to move into two congregations, the second one being nearer to central Brighton. Then they had further multiplied to five, and I was asked to take the lead of the congregation in the Hove building, the only building that the church owned at that time. The other four congregations met in rented premises. This arrangement was different to multi-site churches that have sprung up in a number of places more recently. The most obvious difference was that all five congregations met together one Sunday a month, usually at Hove Town Hall. Terry would often preach at these combined celebrations.

My start at Hove was quite challenging. I soon realised that the move to five congregations had taken a lot of planning and organisation, but all of that had been directed towards the three new congregations. At Hove, there had been very little thought given to the congregation, which in a way, had been left behind twice as the other congregations were planted. The children's work was in some disarray, there was no administrator, and the congregation seemed to feel somewhat bereft as a large number of people had peeled off to help make up the new congregations. The excitement was found in the new groups, whereas we had been left to get on with it! There was also a rather strange positioning of elders. Upon my arrival at the church, there were seven full-time elders in total and four part-time elders. Each congregation was led by a full-time elder, but mine had the addition of three non-full-time elders. Nigel Ring, who was Terry's administrator and acted as an elder to the whole church, also attended my congregation. Terry remained lead elder for the whole church, and David Fellingham, with his great musical abilities, songwriting skills and strong prophetic gifting, was thought to be best suited to input across all five congregations. David was also superb in a crisis, so he helped across the congregations if there was a major pastoral crisis. It was a bit complicated; I must admit, in my earliest days, I had moments when I wondered, 'What on earth have I come to!'

My initial task was to regather the congregation at Hove, put in some structure, and get to know my part of the flock. With all the changes, the three non-full-time Elders with me knew that some effort was needed to motivate the congregation through a new season. However, we formed a friendship and started to work together well, although there were only to be twenty months before the next major change.

I remained in the church eldership for twenty-three years, which I count as one of the great privileges of my life. It was a fantastic team. During the course of those years, I served alongside seventeen other elders in total; six of us were together for that whole period. I retired in 2009, and the last of the six, Steve Walford, retired in 2022, having been an elder for about thirty-eight years. I doubt that record will ever be exceeded in the Brighton Church. The harmony and unity of the team was outstanding for all the years that I was involved.

One of the very positive contributions of the church in Brighton has been the number of members that have moved on to help with church plants or to lead other churches, and that was also true of the elders that left the team during my time there. John Wilthew, who, like me, had once been a Baptist Pastor, moved to help lead the team at the Newfrontiers church in Sidcup before moving on again to plant a new church in Northumberland. Marshall Schaitel moved to the South West to lead a church in Exmouth before he moved again to Norfolk, where he has served as an elder in another NewFrontiers church and also taught in local schools. Peter Lyndon, who as an elder headed up so much of our social action, moved to a church in Manchester and served on the leadership team there while giving help to other churches involved in social action. Peter Brooks, who was our youth leader for a time, then became an elder before taking the role of lead elder in our church, decided, in his mid-forties, to return to his native Australia and led a church in Sydney for some years. Later he changed roles to work as a school counsellor as well as being involved in another church in Sydney. There were other church members who moved on to become elders and sometimes lead elders in churches in Bristol, Birmingham, Leicester, Hull, Bedford, Poole, Truro, Ipswich, Horsham, Darlington, Bath, Christchurch in New Zealand, Accra in Ghana, Montpellier in France and churches in southern Spain. Even that will not be the full list.

Difficulties

In Brighton, we did face one major difficulty in my early years on the eldership team.

About 18 months after I joined the team, Terry suggested that the full-time elders have a short retreat together. We booked a country house in rural Sussex and spent two or three days there. When it came to discussing strategy, I said I'd like us to discuss our present five congregation arrangement. My conviction was that the five congregations felt like five small churches and robbed us of the sense of being a big church in a well-known town (we were granted city status later). The congregations gave more opportunity for contributions in our worship times – something we were very strong on – but they lacked the energy which a large number of people celebrating together creates. Broken down into five congregations, we seemed to have lost some momentum. We tossed this to and fro, but it was obvious that there was an increasing conviction that we would demonstrate our oneness best by being all together every Sunday. This was more than a conclusion to a long discussion; our conviction was that it felt good to the Holy Spirit and us. (Acts 15:28). There was a real rise of excitement among us, and we agreed that we would need to find a building to rent every Sunday which could accommodate hundreds of people and also allow us to run a crèche and children's work. This would give Dave Fellingham the opportunity to pull the musicians together from across the congregations and organise bands for each Sunday while the present lead elders from the congregations would share the preaching with Terry. In practise, 3 or 4 of us went on to do most of the preaching. The other thing we needed to do, of course, was to share this with the non-full-time elders. That's when we hit a real difficulty.

Back in Brighton, we met with the part-time elders who served alongside us and shared our thinking. One of them immediately agreed with the decision and soon stepped down from the eldership team as he felt that with so many of us, it would be top-heavy when we were meeting back together as one church. He and his wife went on to serve the church magnificently for many years, well into retirement. The three elders from my congregation weren't happy about what we shared with them and felt that they should have been included in the original conversation. I believe they had a valid point. They were fully church elders, and we presented them with a decision we'd made without involving them at all. We were wrong about that. We had a number of subsequent conversations with them, sometimes all together and sometimes individually, but we were unable to reach a meeting of minds between us. A decision had to be made, and Terry believed it was right for us to go ahead with what we had decided when away. A little later, the three men felt that for them, the right course of action after these difficulties was for them to leave the church.

Fortunately, that was not the end of the story. It was probably about two years later that I was preaching on spiritual warfare. The three men who had left us were well known and respected across the whole church, and so it had upset people when they left. I felt it was time to address it directly in my sermon. From Ephesians 6:11, where Paul warns Believers to be aware of the devil's schemes, I pointed out that Satan wants to attack the church. His master plan is always to cause division among God's people, and we need to be aware of that. I then made direct reference to the elders who had left us. I pointed out they were really good men, and in all the discussions we'd had together, none of us ever said that our disagreements were due to a character failing. We all wanted the best for the church. I pointed out that the issue we had disagreed on was a genuine one, but as you looked at it objectively, it should have been easy enough to sort out. Why couldn't we do that? I suggested we'd all been caught out by the devil's schemes and forgotten Paul's warning. Why had things always gotten worse when we talked together? It now seemed crazy that we hadn't resolved it. I said I believed that without any of us realising it, the devil had got on the back of our discussions and driven us to a point where we didn't seem to be able to agree. How sad we hadn't realised what was happening.

What didn't cross my mind was that the sermon was being recorded. In those days, recordings were run off on small cassettes, and you could get one at the end of the service. I found out later that several of the congregation had taken cassettes of the sermon and posted them through the letterboxes of these ex-elders. But that proved to be a turning point. The three men listened to the message and realised that they, too, had been caught out, with us, by the devil's schemes. What followed was a true reconciliation. Two of them rejoined the church a little later, and the third continued in a leadership role in another local church but remained in good fellowship with us until years later when he also rejoined. For years after that, whenever I talked to leaders about eldership, I told this story and stressed that if some of their elders were full-time and some were not, it's vital to make the big decisions together. We must be aware that the devil looks to cause division, and to have a two-tier eldership gives him an easy foothold.

The Big Picture

The place we found to rent and meet together in on a Sunday morning was the Odeon Cinema in central Brighton. It was a multi-screen Cinema, and the main theatre seated 900. There were smaller theatres where we held our children's meetings. A good-sized lounge area served well for a crèche. The Cinema's position, its size and the separate theatre spaces were all positive features. On the downside, the children's areas were quite dark, and meeting in a rented space meant we had to set up everything from scratch for the service each week, and we had to finish on time. Our meetings could run more than one and a half hours, and afterwards, we might have a time of prayer with some of the congregation. We then had to dismantle all the gear we had taken into the cinema and make sure we were out before the first showing of the current film! There were a few times when it was a very close call. Some Sunday mornings, there were rather lurid posters on the walls of the crèche area, advertising a forthcoming film. The babies might not have been shocked, but a young mum walking in with her newborn for the first time might have flinched. We had to be somewhat creative in disguising some of those posters. One of the biggest problems was the cost: £1000 per week and this was in 1988. Inevitably this led us to consider how long we should continue to meet there and whether we could find a new building that we could purchase as our own. This consideration developed into a conviction that we should look to buy a new venue, and then £1000 a week for rent seemed like money which we ought to be saving. That caused us to make another change, and we went back to our own building in Hove and held repeat meetings in the morning and evening.

It was remarkable how flexible the congregation was in the face of all this change. Over a few short years, the church had moved from one to two congregations to five congregations, then returned to one congregation in a Cinema and then to morning and evening congregations back in Hove. For some very long-term members, there were still two more moves to take place. I can't claim that no one ever complained about all this change, but I never remember hearing sustained criticism of all the moving around. Nor can I recall people leaving us because they were fed up with the changes. People did leave us for various reasons, but not because we changed venues. We once had a Prayer Meeting where a visiting pastor brought us a prophetic word about us being a pilgrim people. For us to move on, yet again, was something that we embraced in a positive way believing that God didn't want us to stand still, and if we saw the cloud move, then we packed up once again and followed.

Over the years, we had a number of people who did leave us and joined other local churches. This was interesting because when Clarendon Church was in its early stages, there were many complaints that we were taking people away from other churches. With the charismatic movement and the formation of new churches in its wake, together with the message of a restoration of the church that was being spread through the Bible weeks and Conferences, there undoubtedly was some movement of people from more traditional churches to the new ones. But after some years, this settled down, and we reached a point where people were leaving us just as much as people were joining us from other fellowships. I've always been inquisitive about why people would leave us. I remember once asking a local Vicar who'd seen a number of our people move to his church why he thought that it was happening. He responded by saying that he felt people got weary of constant revolution. This didn't appear to have anything to do with the change of buildings but more with the change in how we organised the life of the church; this may have been particularly true with regard to our small groups. It may have seemed at times that we were constantly reorganising, though I would hardly have called it a revolution.

Another reason that individuals sometimes gave for leaving was that the church was too big. I have yet to meet a pastor who doesn't want his church to grow, so to hear that we were too large was always frustrating. Compared to many churches in other parts of the world, we weren't big at all, even if we were in a UK setting. Then again, think what the church will be like in heaven when those gathered around the throne will be too great a multitude to count! Still, there were those who felt they wanted to be somewhere small enough for everyone to know everybody else. We never really cracked that one, but although our growth rate slowed, people continued to join us in good numbers.

Another Change

In 1989 Sue and I travelled to South Africa for four months to work with a church in Cape Town. By the time we returned, we had been part of Clarendon Church for three years, and I could see, coming back after a time away, that Terry was overstretched in terms of both leading the church as well as keeping up with an ever-expanding ministry. He was in great demand not only in the UK but also overseas and really didn't have the time to give his own church the leadership it needed. Having been away, I could see that the church and elders seemed a bit stuck. I knew I must speak to Terry about this, but I was nervous about doing so because I thought it might look as though I was asking to take the lead myself. It was obvious to me that if there was a change of leadership, I would certainly be in the running to take that role. Anyway, I did speak to him, and Terry immediately agreed it was time for him to pass the leadership to someone else. That is how I became the lead elder at Clarendon Church.

Chapter 7

Leading CCK

Shortly after I became the lead elder of the church, we identified a new building when a warehouse quite close to the centre of Brighton came on the market. We agreed to pay £650,000, knowing that renovations and alterations would cost a great deal more, not least because the building was on two levels, and we wanted three. The existing roof was flat and had been built strongly enough to be used as a car park. We saw that this could serve as the floor for another storey which would then itself be covered with a new lightweight roof. The plan was to make the top floor a large open space as the main meeting room for the church, and the two lower floors would be divided up for youth, children, reception and other breakout rooms. Our initial thoughts had been for a building that might cost around a million pounds; it eventually cost three and a half million. (Since then, when I've talked to a leader from another church about how much they would be thinking of spending on new premises that they were hoping to buy, I've always said, 'treble your first number,' and usually, I've been proved right). As a church, we were now facing a major construction project and, therefore, the need to raise a very large sum of money. We decided to give away 10% of all that was given to the building project, which meant that over the years, we donated hundreds of thousands of pounds to mission and to the care of the poor.

Giving

It took us more than ten years to clear the debt, but we had some very exciting gift days and answers to prayer on the way. A few of these have really stuck in my mind. For our first gift day, we didn't set a target; we just wanted a lot of money! When, on the Sunday evening following the offering in the morning service, we received news that the total was £250,000, we were somewhat overwhelmed, grateful to God, thankful for the generosity of the people, and we knew we were off to a good start.

Our church administrator had an interesting time when depositing the cash into a new account with a Building Society. He made it clear that we were a local church that wanted to open an interest-bearing account for some of our money, and this was accepted in a routine, even slightly bored fashion by the assistant at the desk. When the question was asked: 'How much do you wish to deposit to open the account,' and the answer was '£250.000,' suddenly a door was opened with an invitation, 'would you like to come in and have a coffee with the Manager?'

One evening we had what I've always thought of as our Adullam's cave prayer meeting. In 1 Samuel 22, David, fearing for his life, fled from the presence of King Saul to a cave at a place called Adullam. We read that he was joined there by those who were in distress or in debt, or discontented. These unlikely warriors gathered for David and his cause. As a church, we had reached a point where we wanted to take possession of the new building debt free before we started the renovation work. We still owed £30,000 and called a prayer meeting about this. I looked at those who came and, in all honesty, felt very discouraged. Almost everyone there looked as though they were in debt or distressed. There were a good number of students, and an unusually high number of single mothers were present, both demographics being those with real constraints on their finances. I thought this wasn't a £30,000 prayer meeting. But, we asked God. The following Sunday, we took up the offering, and the total came to almost exactly £30,000. We felt that the people were with us and with our cause.

In the autumn of 1999, when we had been in the building for some years, as elders, we believed that it would be great to clear the remaining money that we owed and enter the new millennium with everything paid. Our gift day was in October, and Terry Virgo suggested that we not only ask for money that day but also for pledges that would be redeemed by the end of the year. So we received about half the money needed on the gift day itself, and the pledges edged us towards the £300,000. So we prayed that we could close the gap. On the 31st of December 1999, we had £301,000 in the bank. We rejoiced greatly.

The Building

Besides the financial adventure that we were on with the Building Fund, there were some interesting associated events. We needed planning permission for the change of use of the building from a retail outlet to a place of worship. Brighton Council were opposed to this and unanimously rejected our application. Their argument was that the building could still be used in such a way as to give people a place of employment there. The local television news interviewed Terry about this, and he affirmed his belief that we would get permission. There was an appeal to a government planning officer, and he upheld our application. This was the first time a planning decision which had been unanimously rejected by the Brighton Council had been overturned.

Later we made a rather different appeal, which went to the House of Lords about a VAT charge. This was a highly technical matter to do with whether the building was, in effect, a new build project or the alteration of an old building. There were grey areas about this. We were charged a very large sum for VAT but believed the tax was wrongly applied. Again it became a rather technical matter. The House of Lords doesn't sit in a full session to hear this kind of case, but it is decided by a couple of their judges. Ours was the second of two very similar appeals to be heard on the same day, and whatever happened to the first appeal would mean that ours would be dealt with in the same way. On the day itself, a judge failed to turn up, which by default meant a positive verdict for the first appeal and so for ours as well. Another victory!

As elders, we faced another big challenge when we were suddenly presented with a very large price increase for the new roof and the work to be done on the top floor. During earlier stages of the building work, we decided that we could meet in the building before the top floor was constructed. The ground floor work was finished, so we could accommodate the children safely, and we then held the main Sunday meeting on the first floor before any work was done there, though we cleared everything out of it to allow us to arrange the seating. The builders were brilliant and completed all the work on the floor above without us ever having to leave the building. Unexpectedly we were confronted with an estimate of £1,000,000 for the top floor work when originally we had been led to believe the figure would be much lower. As the lead elder, I felt the burden of having to go back to the church and tell them we wanted a lot more money. We even discussed whether we should abandon our plans for the top floor and continue to use the other two floors and end the project there. There was a lack of peace in the room as we discussed all of this without coming to a clear decision. We decided to stop talking, all go for a walk on our own and come back an hour later with some fresh thinking. It's a big claim to say you believe God has spoken to you when you face a very big decision, but I believe he did. As I walked around, I received a really strong conviction that we should tell the church our vision and not present the money as the issue. The elders were at one with this, and that's what happened. The next Sunday, I cancelled a visit I was going to make to another church and stood on the platform in my own church and, as best I could, spelt out our vision for the use of the building. The money did get mentioned, but from then on, it never seemed a big deal; what we were convinced of was that we needed to finish the building work and use what God had given us for his mission and glory.

As the building work progressed above us and we were now meeting on what had become the middle floor, it was getting dustier by the week. We had a carpet covering over bare concrete, and the dust was settling into that, and then some of the lights began to go out, and the whole area was getting dingier and dirtier. When the day came when we could leave that floor and move upstairs, I suggested a celebration service. We held what we called the: Goodbye Middle Floor Celebration. There was enthusiastic worship, dancing and much general celebration, which included lots of balloons. All of this moving around so stirred up the dust and dirt that by the end of the meeting, there was a thick mist, and we could hardly see one end of the hall from the other. I could only hope that it didn't give any vulnerable individuals a severe asthma attack. I certainly knew I needed a shower when that meeting was over.

We had one very serious incident during the time we were meeting on the middle floor. Late one evening, the building alarm went off, and this was picked up at home by our church administrator. He and others went down to the building, checked the meeting hall and found no sign of a break-in. They checked the door to a small balcony that was on the middle floor, but it was firmly locked, so there was obviously no one there either. The next morning when a member of the church staff went in, they discovered there had been a break-in. There was serious damage to the PA desk, and a lot of the chairs had been thrown around and bent out of shape; it was quite a mess. What had happened was that a man had hidden in the building after a meeting had finished and when the building was closed up he climbed onto the balcony and so when the door was checked it was locked, and it was assumed that no one was in there. After the building had been checked following the alarm, he went to work. The police were able to trace the individual who'd done this, a man with very serious mental health issues who sometime later, very sadly, committed suicide.

The Name

With a new building to meet in, it seemed a good opportunity to think about the name of the church. We easily reached a decision to continue with the Clarendon name for the building, which became the Clarendon Centre, where the church met. But should we change the name of the church itself? It appeared to be easier to accept a million-pound estimate than it did to choose a name. Some of the elders preferred a more geographical name, like *City Church. King's Church* was the choice of some, which was a popular name among NewFrontier's churches as a whole. We really struggled to reach an agreement about this. I even resorted to a vote asking everyone to write down the name they wanted and to see if we could get a majority that way, but that didn't work either. In the end, I decided on a more theological approach. At that time, there was quite a bit of discussion on the way we should understand authority and submission as described in the Bible. I went to Terry and said to him I didn't think we could go on with an endless discussion on the choice of a name, and we needed to settle it by authority and submission. It was either up to him or me to make a choice and for the rest to submit to that. Terry agreed and said he'd make a choice, and that's how we became the *Church of Christ the King*! (This was commonly abbreviated to CCK). Years later, when I was no longer leading the church, we had a rerun of this discussion. We needed to order a complete set of stationery for the church, so if we had any thoughts about changing the name, this would be the time to do it before our name was printed on thousands of pieces of paper. Once again, it was quite a protracted discussion, but we retained the name of the Church of Christ the King. Years later, again and following another change of leadership when Terry's son, Joel, became the Lead Elder and after a number of us had retired, the name was changed to *Emmanuel Church*. There was a special Sunday evening Celebration service which Terry, Dave Fellingham and myself, together with our wives, were all invited to attend. It was a great meeting, but I couldn't help thinking that Terry, Dave and I were all sitting there and saying to ourselves, 'Well, I wouldn't have chosen this name!' However, I believe that Joel was right when he said you could make too little of a name or too much of a name. Mind you, my wife has sometimes heard a surname that she doesn't like and told me she wouldn't have married me if I'd had that name, but then perhaps she would.

John Piper

I can't remember any time in my life when I met someone who would be considered really famous. Living through the whole of the reign of Queen Elizabeth 11, I never got anywhere near seeing her in person. However, I have spent a day with one very well-known Christian leader, preacher and writer, and that was John Piper. I've probably appreciated his books as much as any Christian literature I've studied. Terry had been able to arrange for John Piper to speak to NewFrontier's leaders in our building in Brighton over the course of a couple of days. Before the conference, John and his wife Noel had a free day, and Terry was unable to meet up with them until the evening. He asked if Sue and I could entertain them for the day. It was a fascinating few hours talking with them, but during that time, I thought I'd show John Piper where he would be speaking the next day, so I took him into our building. On display in the main hall was the complete range of John Piper's books so that those attending could purchase any that they wanted. John said, 'I'm surprised to see that you've got all my books here.' To which I quipped in reply, 'Oh, we wanted to help you with your royalties.' This was one of those occasions when I really wished I'd kept my mouth shut. The next morning I was sitting in the front row while John Piper was speaking, and he mentioned the book display. 'I'd just like to explain,' he said, 'That I don't receive any royalties from these books, which all go to the work of missions.' I felt like crawling under the seat. I've seen on some websites that John Piper's wealth is estimated to be in the region of twenty-five million dollars. That's rubbish; his fortune has gone into world mission.

Family

During our years at the Church of Christ the King, our older son, Matthew, attended sixth-form college, while our younger son, David, attended a local Catholic Comprehensive school. Matthew spent a year in southern Africa before attending Newcastle University, which is where he met Grace, who was visiting the city with a friend. I married them in our original building in Hove before they moved to Canterbury for a short time. David met his wife, Emma, during the time of his University studies in Southampton, though she was a member of our church. I later married them in our new building, although on this occasion, Matthew preached. David and Emma lived for a time in Brighton before moving to Sidcup, followed by four years in America working with Bank of America and then returned to Sidcup to continue working with the same Bank but based in central London. Over the course of these years, we became grandparents to seven grandchildren, six girls and one boy.

These were also the years when our parents grew old and died. Sue's stepfather, whom her mother had married ten years after being widowed, went very suddenly with a heart attack. Sue's mother spent some time in a nursing home in Brighton before slipping away in her mid-nineties after we cut short a visit to South Africa. Sue was with her for a few hours before she died. We faced a few complications with my parents, who had retired to Cornwall. My father appeared to be the frail one, while my mother seemed in remarkably good health. However, she very suddenly developed cancer of the liver and died ten weeks after her diagnosis. There were several long journeys to Cornwall to visit her during those last few weeks, and we had to find a nursing home for my father when my mother went into a Hospice for her final few days. We had one very traumatic day when we delivered my mother to the Hospice and, an hour later, my father to the nursing home before returning on a dark, cold night to Brighton. After my mother's death, we were able to bring my father to a nursing home near Brighton, where he died just over a year later.

After I had led the Brighton Church for about six years, Terry and Wendy Virgo moved to America for two years to help a church there. It was a time when Terry was also able to see the emergence of some American churches that wished to relate to him through the growing NewFrontiers network of churches. We kept in close contact during that time, and I have kept on file some very warm correspondence that Terry sent me during that period as we exchanged news about what was happening. Terry and Wendy's return to Brighton was to trigger another major change in our lives.

Chapter 8

Ephesians 4

During the early years of the Bible weeks known as 'The Dales' and 'The Downs,' it was sometimes stated that if you asked the congregation to open their Bibles, they would automatically fall open at Ephesians 4. This was because of the amount of teaching given around verses 11 and 12, which read: 'So Christ himself gave the apostles, the prophets, the evangelists, the pastors and teachers, to equip his people for works of service, so that the body of Christ might be built up....'

Although most Christians at the time were familiar with evangelists, and pastors and teachers, there was a general belief that apostles and prophets had died out with the New Testament era. This was particularly true with regard to apostles owing to verses that suggest that a qualification for that ministry was to be an eyewitness to the resurrected Christ, and you can't move on too far from the event for that to remain possible. But many of us became persuaded by other Biblical arguments that there were men in every generation who had functioned as apostles and that they, along with the prophets and other ministries, were gifts of the ascended Christ to the church in every age. These complementary ministries have a very clear purpose, which is stated in the Ephesians 4 passage; to equip the body of Christ for the service of God. Apostles are able to lay foundations; prophets can stir up the people of God; evangelists can help the church in the work of sharing the gospel; pastors and teachers care for and teach the body of Christ. Around a similar time, many Believers became convinced that we need all these ministries to help the church function as it should.

There was a lesser point that was often discussed as to whether 'pastors and teachers' were two distinct ministries or whether they were two aspects of one ministry. My vote definitely went with the latter, as it seems to me that if you teach people without pastoring them, you are simply a lecturer, but if you pastor people without teaching them, you can very easily become simply a 'there, there's sort of person - lots of sympathy but little content. I would say that generally, in the UK, we would tend to talk about a fourfold ministry, but in South Africa, where I travelled often, it was usually spoken of as a fivefold ministry.

Commonly these ministries have been referred to as 'the Ephesians 4 ministries.' I have always struggled with that title, fearing it could be elitist. Sometimes when I was a visiting preacher, I was introduced as an Ephesians 4 pastor and teacher. I used to think about other excellent elders and wondered whether some of them would be regarded as Ephesians 2 pastors or teachers. Of course, Paul never wrote Ephesians as chapters and verses; it was divided up like that later for ease of reference. Paul wouldn't have understood the term Ephesians 4 ministries! However, in Ephesians 4, we read of ministries that the ascended Christ gave to the church, and all have a contribution to make to the health of the church.

Terry Virgo was certainly recognised to have the ministry gift of an 'apostle'. Alongside Terry's own sense of call about this, and that is certainly not to be overlooked, his ability to inspire church planting, to help churches be transformed into a greater likeness to the New Testament model, to lay doctrinal foundations into a local church and then to oversee an ever-growing number of leaders spoke for itself. A large number of leaders trusted Terry enough to want to be joined into the network that he was overseeing. Even outside of NewFrontiers, other leaders have often looked to him for help and advice and would invite him to speak at their conferences. It was, therefore, with Terry's apostolic gift that the NewFrontiers family of churches began to grow, although the other ministries were also recognised as having a crucial role.

I've sometimes thought about Terry's gifting, which, although it can be described to some extent, and I'm going to attempt that, somehow transcends description. I believe I got an insight into this years ago when I read an article in a Christian leadership magazine about a pastor in America who was invited to take the lead of a 5,000-member mega-church. His predecessor, apparently, just became weary of leading such a large church and decided to step away. Over the next few years, the new pastor watched the church decline to about 2000 before it levelled off. His own analysis was interesting. He wrote that there were large numbers among the 5000, who never really had any personal contact with their previous pastor, but he had a gift, call it an anointing, that meant that everyone in the congregation would say, 'That's my pastor.' The new pastor simply said, 'I didn't have that gift.' Similarly, although not every leader in NewFrontiers had close personal contact with Terry, though they would definitely have friendships with other leaders in NewFrontiers, he had that ability to instil confidence and trust in a wide number of leaders.

I did have a lot of personal contact with Terry for over 20 years. Apart from my wife, no one has impacted my life as much as he.

Terry's Impact

Terry always conveys a very strong sense of security in God. His belief in the sovereignty of God, that God has spoken authoritatively through his Word and that God is committed to our good, whatever the circumstances, are truths he constantly communicates. Above all, he was gripped by the grace of God and often taught and preached on this. This sense of security was always evident to me in the way that I never saw him come anywhere near to panic, even though there were some very demanding situations that he sometimes had to deal with. He always gave a calm, measured response. You could tell he trusted God.

His handling of prophecy also underlined his confidence in God. He had a remarkable ability to remember prophetic words. If Terry heard a prophecy and believed God was giving some direction through it, he could quote it years later and act upon it. There were a number of these prophecies that became quite key in our development as a family of churches, but nothing that Terry acted on was ever wild or weird. Overall, it was his sense of security in God that helped so many of us who were in the leadership of churches also to feel greater security.

Over the years, I've often read or heard of someone described as a man or woman of prayer and have wondered how exactly that would be measured. To know Terry was genuinely to know a man of prayer. He never paraded it, but it leaked out of his private life and devotions. Working with him over the years, I heard enough passing comments to realise the absolute priority of personal prayer in his own life. When interacting with us as a team of elders, prayer was always the priority. I'm not sure he exactly taught us how to pray, for the team was pretty mature anyway, but he certainly inspired us to pray. This, of course, fed into our church life as a whole. The Brighton Church was a prayerful church. Sure, we could have been more prayerful, but Terry's lead certainly inspired us. Before I joined the Brighton Church, I'd attended so many prayer meetings where there would be long pauses with no one praying. That never happened when Terry was in a prayer meeting. He prayed in a way that would fire up others to pray as well. Perhaps sometimes he was a bit too dominant in a prayer meeting, and I know from a conversation that I once had with him that he recognised that, but he certainly inspired others to seek God. Three times a year, he hosted two days of Prayer and Fasting gatherings for all NewFrontiers leaders. I think the first time I attended one of these at Pilgrim Hall Christian Centre in Sussex, there were about 70 present. Years later, we met in Peterborough with 600-800 present. They often felt like powerful times of encounter with God and were strategic in helping us forward as a movement of churches.

Terry was also a great preacher. He could be very pastoral when preaching to the local church. In my early days at Brighton, he could also be a bit long, especially in his introductions. He asked me once to comment on his preaching, and I made that observation which he really seemed to take note of. I know that you can listen to a good preacher for a good length of time, but whereas at a Bible Week meeting, you would certainly expect and even want a message that lasted for an hour, that becomes quite a long time regularly on a Sunday. I would say that the pattern for all the preachers at Brighton settled down to about 45 minutes, which might still be considered a long sermon by many today but was expected in the church there. When it came to preaching to leaders, Terry was usually superb. I have never listened to anyone better at addressing leadership issues or inspiring leaders to press on in building the church. I think for many people, their testimony to Terry's influence on their life would be in the way they have come more fully to understand the grace of God. For myself, although grace was important, what really kept me riveted with Terry's teaching was his ability to inspire me with a vision for the church. At the Bible Weeks we held at the Downs in Sussex and then later at Stoneleigh in the Midlands, Terry was world-class when addressing congregations of thousands. A number of times, he preached about an Old Testament character, and his series of messages on Joseph and Nehemiah stands out as particularly memorable. I was profoundly impacted when Terry spoke one year to a leader's seminar at one of the Bible Weeks on Paul's visit to Ephesus from Acts 19. A visiting, highly gifted speaker himself commented afterwards that he was amazed at what Terry got out of the text. His preaching could be like that, you'd think, 'Is that really in the passage?' and yes, it was, but he managed to point out what you somehow hadn't seen before. When the season for the Bible Weeks concluded, and we held Leaders Conferences in Brighton, I can recall Terry giving an outstanding series of expositions on Ephesians. There are a few preachers who have made a real impact on my life, and Terry is right up there.

Another dimension of Terry's ministry was his wisdom. He was able to assess situations and comment on or teach them in a way that was consistently helpful. In 1994 there was considerable excitement in churches about what was called the 'Toronto Blessing', which began in Canada and went worldwide. There was a lot of phenomena connected with this (people falling over when they were prayed for, and a lot more besides). This raised real questions about how we handled it all, what could be accepted and what perhaps should be rejected. I remember Terry addressing this in one of the Bible Week sessions with real insight and wisdom and giving such practical help with all that was happening.

God raises up leaders, and so many of us over the years have been grateful that God raised up Terry with the integrity, gifting and anointing that has been of such help, especially, I would say, to very many church leaders.

Change Again

I've had a number of conversations over the years about the admiral on the ship. I was the first lead elder in Newfrontiers to face this, but with the emergence of other apostolic ministries, this was repeated a few times elsewhere. Those who develop an apostolic ministry have almost certainly already been leading their own church. With widening responsibilities, it becomes necessary to pass the leadership to someone else in the team while often remaining as part of the local team. Using the metaphor of the lead elder as captain of the ship; then the apostle becomes like an admiral on board with responsibility for a whole number of churches.

Inevitably there come times when the admiral and the captain don't see eye to eye on something. For some years, we ran a prayer meeting early on Saturday mornings. This began with very good numbers, but over the years began slowly to decline and started to run out of steam. One of the things I learned about prayer meetings at Brighton was that there is wisdom in changing the pattern of them from time to time. I noticed that these meetings always began with a lot of life but would eventually become a bit stale, and then we would make a change. Terry was particularly committed to our Saturday prayer meetings. He was away when I decided to change the pattern. When he returned, the change was already made, and he simply didn't agree with it. I share this as a typical example of an admiral-captain clash that can occur when the admiral is on board. My big mistake, and it was a big one, was not to talk this over with Terry before making the decision. In my opinion, Terry's mistake was a failure to accept that, as captain, I was more aware of the day-to-day running of the ship and how it was working than he was. We had to resolve it, and we did, but there was some pain for both of us on that one.

While I was leading the church, Terry spent two years in America, and a number of the UK pastors believed that he would remain there, though; personally, I never did. At one point during those years, Terry addressed a leader's meeting back in the UK and mentioned something that would happen when he returned permanently. There was a loud burst of laughter around the room, which was actually communicating the widespread belief: you won't be coming back to the UK, Terry. He was visibly shocked and insisted that he would return, which indeed he did.

If a week is a long time in politics, then two years is a very long time in a family of churches. Terry returned to find that life had moved on. David Holden, who was based at the Sidcup Church and had always worked closely with Terry from the days when he was in Seaford, had taken the lead in the UK while Terry was away, and inevitably, there had been a number of changes. How easy was it for Terry to pick up the leadership again? Probably not easy at all in the first few months, and Terry had to re-establish his ministry to some extent. At this point, he felt that it would be the right way forward if he was to lead the Brighton Church again. He didn't ask me to step down as such, but I could see which way the wind was blowing. We discussed my taking on a wider teaching role and then communicated to the elders and the church that there was to be a change. The following year proved to be a bit unsettling. Churches don't always immediately hear what is being communicated, especially perhaps larger churches. Very often, something has to be repeated several times before it is really understood. Over the next few months, I realised that a whole number of church members thought I was still leading the church despite what we had told them. Also, Terry's gift and ministry meant that very quickly, the calls upon his time and input ramped up again. The situation was beginning to parallel the time prior to my becoming lead elder when Terry simply didn't have the time to give to the local church. This got resolved a year later when Peter Brooks, another of the eldership team, was appointed to lead the church.

During this time, I did have one very lonely moment. A few weeks after the change had been made, I was in my study and gradually realised that none of the other elders were around. Obviously, I enquired about this only to find that Terry had taken the rest of the team away for a couple of days for a short retreat and discussions. It was a time (and we had many of these times) when there was a lot of talk about re-organising and resetting our small group program. As my role had now changed to a wider one, Terry saw no reason to include me in this very local discussion. That was reasonable enough, but at the time, I felt pretty devastated and left out after eight years of leading the team and church.

My wife and I often quote a Chinese saying; all change is loss. Obviously, I did feel a certain amount of loss, having led the church for those years and then not doing so. At the same time, there was to be a great deal of gain. I would be able to develop the training programs that I'd become increasingly involved with and also to travel much more widely. So for the next twelve or thirteen years, I was to spend about one-third of my time at Brighton continuing to preach there very regularly. I spent another third of my time around the UK involved in leader's training and also preaching and teaching at other churches. The other third of my time involved ministry overseas, and with our two sons having left home and married, it meant that Sue was often able to travel with me. I am extremely grateful for the experience and opportunity of those years. I am also very conscious that it was only because of Terry's ministry that those opportunities came my way. None of it would have happened without the existence of NewFrontiers of which he was the founding father, and none of it would have happened unless he had released me to take on that wider role. So once again, Terry had a huge impact on my life.

Chapter 9

Change of Role

With less responsibility in the Brighton church, I was able to give more attention to our leadership training courses. Over the years, there had been some evolution of these programs as the number of churches that had become part of NewFrontiers continued to grow. What had once been a central training course to which everyone came was now becoming more regionalised as bases were established in London, Norwich, Sheffield and Brighton. I began to develop a general oversight of these bases and did some teaching in each of them while also being particularly responsible for the Brighton base. We agreed to establish a 'national curriculum', so it was necessary for me to call together the base leaders from time to time to keep a check on this and also to agree on various organisational practices.

The Foundations Course was typical of what might be found in a Bible College. It included Christian doctrine, church history, the character of leaders, time management, and Old Testament and New Testament studies. What it didn't include was much in the way of Biblical exegesis. I am sure that in my years at Spurgeon's College, I had not even heard the word 'hermeneutics' referring to the interpretation of Scripture, but over the years, this had clearly become the key subject for Christian leaders to give attention to. I believed we needed to address this with our own training. So we developed a new two-year course, which we called 'Advanced', to follow on from our Foundations Course. This was almost completely committed to the exegesis of a number of books of the Bible. We also emphasised the place of preaching as we really wanted those who were preachers to attend the course. We kept the numbers limited to a maximum of 15 in each base in order to allow plenty of personal interaction and conversation. Over a number of years, this proved to be very popular, probably because preachers love to work through the actual text of the Bible.

At the time, I was the only one teaching Hebrews, and on one occasion, we brought the Brighton and Norwich bases together so that I could teach both at the same time. Walking into the room to teach on the first day, I realised that I was faced with a larger group that included four men with First Class Honours degrees, one of whom had already obtained a higher degree for studies in Hebrews. I wondered how I was going to cope. Whenever we approached any of the really challenging passages (for example, the warning passage of Hebrews 6, which raised endless debates as to whether we can lose our salvation), I broke them into small groups to discuss the passage before I taught on it. I would always put these four guys together, then stand back to watch the sparks fly!

Writing

During these years, I was able to write three books. I had given some teaching on The End Times at a Bible Week seminar where an employee of a Christian book company approached me and asked whether I would think of writing a book on the subject. I agreed to send him some of my lecture material and received an invitation to turn that material into a book they could publish. I did this but with a very tight deadline set by the publishers. So they printed: 'The End Times' and then reprinted it. I wished afterwards that I'd asked for a longer writing time and could have done a better job of it.

The same publishers then approached me to consider writing for them again. I had done some lecturing on the Book of Revelation to the Advanced groups and had also preached through it in the Brighton Church. My hope was to make what seemed to be a difficult book accessible to everyone. I was also keen to avoid sensational interpretations, which can easily happen with this book, so I made sure to research the best evangelical commentaries available thoroughly. I always make the point that I have nothing original to say about the book of Revelation, but I hoped my book: 'The Lamb, the Beast and the Devil' would make it less intimidating to read. I've felt this was the best of my three books.

The third book was 'Christ's Radiant Church', which came about because I was aware that I'd often been asked what it was that made our churches distinctive. Why did there need to be NewFrontiers when there were already a multitude of Christian denominations? So I wrote the book to explain what we had found important to emphasise in church life. It's not comprehensive; for example, there is no chapter on the Lord's Supper, but there are things that we believed God had led us to emphasise in the new churches we were building.

Travels

Naturally, what I had lectured on and written about was sometimes reflected in seminars that I gave in local churches. This means I have done a lot of teaching on the End Times and the Book of Revelation over the years. But I also developed a good relationship with a number of churches across the UK that I used to visit on a regular basis. A couple of times a year, I'd be with the church in Ringwood, once a year with the church in Crawley and once every two years with the church in Keswick in the Lake District. These, together with a number of other churches, meant I had good friendships with the leaders, and I always most enjoyed revisiting churches I knew well. I remember visiting a new church plant in Exeter and speaking to a circle of 12 where one of the ladies with her broken leg in plaster stuck it right into the middle. The group was in the first month of being gathered, the meeting was very informal, and I gave them a choice of two sermons which they voted on. In subsequent years as I revisited this growing church, led by Andy Arscott, my first visit was often referred to, not in terms of the content of the sermon I had preached, but in the way, I'd given them a choice!

To be a regular visiting preacher to a church carries its own dangers, especially since you might inadvertently preach the same sermon twice. I treasure the story told to me by a pastor friend who, before he led a church himself, was a member of a church in Bath. The famous Dr Martyn Lloyd-Jones used to visit each year, midweek, to preach at the church Anniversary, an occasion that was always looked forward to eagerly. My friend told me that the revered Doctor preached the same sermon twice, two years running. But this was a mistake I once made myself.

I was meticulous in keeping a record of what, where and when I had preached in an exercise book that I still possess. One year, in June, I preached a message on the Cross at the church at Heathfield in Sussex. It so happened that in my preaching record, I had left out the month of June, and when I realised this, I inserted it after December. The next year I was asked back during the summer. A lot of the congregation were away on holiday, and also, that particular Sunday, a number of them were at a Christian Conference. I thought to myself, *I'm not going to be casual about this because so many are away; I'll preach my best sermon as though there were hundreds present.* I checked my preaching record to see what I'd preached last time at Heathfield but forgot that I'd confused the months. I preached on the Cross the same message as the year before. It took me some time to live that one down.

Travels Abroad

I had already done a fair amount of travel overseas and especially to South Africa, which I will write about in the next chapter, but this was now to become a very regular part of our lives. For many years I regularly went to India to teach at the NewFrontiers training school in Goa. I had, of course, been to India before when I was in the Merchant Navy, and the accident our ship was involved in meant a stay of nearly two months in Mumbai. That accident was somewhat prophetic of my many visits to Mumbai on my way to Goa. The first time I flew into Mumbai, I was booked to speak at a couple of churches in the city before flying South. As we were landing, the Monsoon rains started, and I stepped out of the airport into what seemed like a waterfall. I was staying for a couple of nights with a young couple who had moved from our church in Brighton to India to start a business and help in a local church. After a restless night listening to the howling wind and lashing rain, I woke to find that hundreds of cockroaches were coming up the steps of the bungalow to escape the flooded road outside. My hosts told me that because of the floods, I would be taken to the building where the church met by one of their young men, but it could involve a lot of walking. The journey proved to be something of a challenge. It involved a rickshaw, but the driver soon gave up because of floodwater and then a short ride on an overcrowded bus until we reached a rail station. Then we had to cross bridges over the tracks where the flood water was level with the platform. Coming out of the station on the other side, things got worse. We were now thigh deep in water, and the young man with me advised that I take care not to fall down a manhole as the covers might well have come off in the road. We walked up this street full of floating cats, mats and dead rats until we reached a block of flats where a church member lived and where we could seek refuge. Needless to say, the Sunday morning meeting was abandoned.

Later in the day, the rain eased off, and I was able to return to the bungalow, but then there was an evening meeting I was due to speak at in another building, though not so far away. The rain started to pour down again, and by now, we were being told it was the heaviest monsoon for many years. Once again, I set off on foot, though this was even scarier as electric pylons had come down in the wind and electricity was arcing across the water in the roads. I arrived at the building and found no one had turned up at all. It was something of a relief when the next day, the weather was much calmer, and I was able to fly down to Goa.

A visit to Mumbai usually coincided with some drama, the least of which was arriving in the middle of the night when there was no one to meet us because they were waiting at a different exit. We spent some very uncomfortable hours in the airport. On another occasion, when I arrived, the Indian government collapsed that day. Coinciding with another arrival, a passenger train was blown up by terrorists. I was due to travel on that line the next day. The most threatening occasion was landing at Mumbai as violence broke out between the Hindu and Muslim communities. While I was preaching that Sunday morning, a man was shot dead outside the building we were meeting in. The next day I was taken by private car to the airport through eerily quiet streets, praying that we wouldn't suddenly turn a corner to be confronted by a rioting mob. I sat in the airport lounge and watched the fires burning in the slums, which reached right up to the airport fence. I was glad to land at the airport in Goa. I asked a pastor friend there whether they ever had violent clashes in their area. 'No, he said, Goans are too lazy to riot!'

My annual visits to India meant I formed some strong friendships there. Many of the men who came through the training program are still leading churches across the nation. It is such a vibrant, exciting, colourful and noisy nation. I loved the Indians and gradually got used to the food. I did have some nasty stomach bugs on my earlier visits, but I think I developed the antibodies to escape them in later years.

One event is seared into my memory from those visits to India. I had been into a shop in Goa and as I came out was holding some small change in my hand. Just as I was getting into a taxi, a small girl approached me. On her hip, she was carrying her totally naked toddler-aged sister. She held out her hand, and I gave her the change I was holding. As soon as the taxi door closed, she was beating on the window with a look of desperation and obviously pleading for more money. As a middle-aged, middle-class visitor, I had assumed she'd be happy that I'd given her some money. In fact, she was desperate for more. I realised I was looking into the face of absolute poverty. I've never forgotten that moment.

Another place Sue and I visited very often was Dubai in the Middle East. Although situated in a Muslim country, Christian churches are generally welcomed as long as they are not attended by the local population. There are many churches in Dubai, and some of them are quite large. The church we were working with was largely made up of Indian, Pakistani and Filipino Believers, plus a few Europeans and South Africans. Sometimes the church met in separate congregations for language reasons, and quite often, there was a change of venue as hotels might rent space for a time and then say we were no longer welcome. I watched the spectacular development of the city during the years we travelled there. On my first visit, I took a photo of the World Trade Centre building as it looked very impressive. In later years, it was to be dwarfed by a multitude of skyscrapers and eventually the Burj Khalifa, which was the tallest building in the world.

We had some excellent times with the church and made some very good friendships. However, in later years, we ran into some heavy weather due to a crisis in the leadership team. This was eventually resolved very successfully, but in the middle of it, my closest friend felt he should step down as an elder and leave the church. I was very upset about this, but I had to have a final meeting with him so he could hand me some keys to a building the church was using at the time. This brought about a serious cross-cultural misunderstanding. Roger was Anglo-Indian and had grown up in India before moving to Dubai to set up a business there. When we said, 'goodbye', I took the keys from him and said, 'Roger, I'm thinking that after seventeen years, we may never see each other again.' From my English perspective, I was expressing deep regret and really some heartfelt grief about the situation. Some months later, I heard that Roger was reporting that I never wanted to see him again. This was, of course, the exact opposite of what I had meant. I spoke to an Indian Believer later, and when I explained what had happened, he told me that from his cultural background, Roger would certainly have heard what I'd said as meaning I didn't want to see him again. I was determined to clear this up and made another couple of visits over the next two years when I got together with Roger. We sorted it out slowly, and our friendship was fully restored. Cross-cultural issues can be complicated.

Over the years, we have also made several visits to the USA, which we enjoyed, but it has never won our hearts in the way India and South Africa did. On one visit during a sabbatical, we were involved with a mega-church that opened its multi-thousand-seat auditorium. On another occasion, we were able to visit Amish communities and see their commitment to a simple lifestyle and very productive farming. We squeezed in a quick visit across the border to Canada to view the magnificent Niagara Falls as well as enjoying a memorable drive around part of the Rockies and their small but enchanting ski resort towns.

We also spent a week at Pensacola in Florida during the time that 'Revival' was taking place there. Many people know that whereas in the UK, we use the word *Revival* to speak of a sovereign and exceptional work of God, in America, the word tends to be used to describe an organised evangelistic crusade. What was happening in the Pensacola Revival was reported to be more like the UK description, and people began to visit from all over the world. It began one Father's Day Sunday morning when a visiting preacher was speaking at the church, and the Spirit of God suddenly fell on the people. There were many deep encounters with God taking place and people's lives being changed. This led to a service being held almost every night for many months, with thousands of people attending and many people testifying to meeting with God. For a week, we joined the queues each evening and were blessed and challenged by being there. Frankly, I would not have described it as Revival in the way I have read of it in the past. The immediate community didn't seem to be affected, and the atmosphere was quite light-hearted compared with the sense of awe at the presence of God that I've read of so often in historical revivals. However, I am sure many people did meet with God, and we certainly returned home spiritually refreshed by our visit there.

The Sunday after we got home, I was preaching at the Brighton Church and, motivated by our time in America, gave it all I had with my preaching in what I refer to as a post-Pensacola passion. Exhausted, I stepped off the platform to be engaged by a sweet lady from our church who immediately addressed me with the words, 'John, do you think you could ask the Alpha catering team only to use free-range eggs? otherwise, it's cruel to the chickens.' That's how to bring a preacher down to earth!

We were fortunate to visit many other nations where I had the opportunity to preach and teach and to see what God is doing through his church around the world. Of these, South Africa was the country with which we most engaged, as I will go on to explain.

Chapter 10

South Africa

My first visit to South Africa was for eight days in February 1987. This involved my first-ever long-haul flight and a whirlwind tour of that amazing country. It slowly dawned on me that this was something of a propaganda trip. A number of Christian leaders had been invited to visit the country to see the opportunities for Christian holiday tours. Terry had been invited, and he asked me to come along as well. It seems likely that the white South African government of the time had financially supported this as it included a visit to Government House in Pretoria, where we were given a very fine lunch and seated alongside some very intellectually smart government employees. Clearly, their job was to tell us about the wonders of South Africa and very deftly to answer any questions about the remaining apartheid system in the country. We were shown the sights in Cape Town, which included a visit to the top of Table Mountain. We stayed in an upmarket hotel in Durban which enabled us to see the spectacular beaches there. A particular highlight was a day and a night in Kruger National Park and a ride out to see the wildlife. It was a highly enjoyable visit, but most significantly, it sowed a seed in my affection for South Africa.

Our real involvement with the country started about two years later. It came about with what I would describe as a real 'God moment.' Early on Friday mornings, we held an elder's prayer meeting. Unusually, Terry brought a letter with him one morning and read it to us. It was from the pastor of the Vineyard Church (later changed to Jubilee Church) in Cape Town. Graham was himself English and wished to take a sabbatical back in the UK. Was there a pastor that Terry could send over to South Africa to lead the church for three months while he was away? Terry told us that he thought that this was very unlikely, and we turned to prayer. Of course, I'd previously visited the country with him, and by the end of the prayer time, I had a burning conviction that I should go. So I took Terry aside to tell him that I thought Sue and I could go. He looked at me and said, 'I suppose you could.' That was a life-altering decision. For the next twenty years, we spent ten percent of our time in South Africa. Our first visit was for four months, and it resulted in major changes for the church there.

At this point, I need to insert another part of our family history. Our older son, Matthew, had decided to take a gap year before going to University and to spend it on a farm in Swaziland in southern Africa. This didn't work out well, so after some months, he joined up with a young man of the same age, also from England, who'd been working on a nearby farm, and they decided to hitchhike down through South Africa. To say the least, this carried some big potential risks, but they made it safely to Cape Town and to the Vineyard Church. Matthew was able to stay on some church property, and his friend returned to England. When we arrived in Cape Town, there was Matthew at the airport waiting to greet us! He didn't return to the UK until shortly after we got back some four months later. Our time there ran right through our English school summer holiday period, so David, who had been staying with friends back in England, was able to join us for the summer holiday period. So for a few weeks, the whole family was in the church together. That proved to be of some significance. Graham, the pastor, was a single guy and really quite eccentric, but he was a great preacher and had built a strong church. However, the fact that we were there as a normal family clearly contrasted with some of Graham's eccentricities and seemed rather to count against him when he returned.

One of the odd things about Graham's behaviour was his attitude towards his elders. He had been unwilling to leave them

91

in charge of the church when he was on sabbatical, which is, of course, how I got there. After some time, I realised those guys would have been more than capable of leading for the three months Graham was away. They knew this, and it didn't exactly make Graham's re-entry an easy one. But there was another twist in the story, which also increased the growing tensions. Prior to Graham's return, a leader's weekend away had been arranged. Not only was I present at this, but David Holden from the UK also arrived, as did Simon Pettit. Simon was the leader of a church in Sussex but believed that God was calling him to South Africa. David already knew South Africa well and wanted to explore with Simon whether Simon could join the team at the Vineyard. David, Simon and I had a couple of rather tense meetings with Graham over the weekend when we discussed the future of the church together. Then something happened, which I only found out about much later. I had an initial talk with David and Simon when I gave a report on my three months with the church. I told them that the elders really wanted Graham to resign and move on. Simon made notes of what I said. Later, in one of the meetings that we had with Graham, he asked if anyone could give him a piece of paper as he wanted to take notes. Simon tore a page out of his notebook, not realising that his notes were on the other side, and gave it to Graham! I can only imagine what Graham thought when he read Simon's notes. In the end, although Sue and I stayed for another month for a holiday, we all left South Africa with nothing clearly decided.

A little later, Terry flew out with Simon to Cape Town to talk with Graham, only to find, on arrival, that Graham had resigned and invited another local pastor to come and take the lead. Typically, Terry believed this wasn't the end of the story. He spent a morning in prayer with Simon, and later in the day, the other church elders turned up to say they didn't want Graham's choice of leader to take over but wanted Simon Pettit to come. Simon coming into lead eldership is why I was able to continue with such a strong link with the church for so many years.

The three full-time elders that had worked closest with Graham left at various stages to lead their own churches but kept in close contact with Simon, who was beginning to develop an apostolic role. Sue and I became very close friends with Jeff and Viv Kidwell, whom Simon encouraged to plant a new church with some members of Jubilee in the area of Muizenburg to the south of Cape Town. This became a large church that grew steadily over the years, as I saw on my regular visits to preach there. Sadly, Viv died at the age of 68, but in retirement, Jeff has continued to serve many local churches in South Africa. We still keep in regular contact. This is simply one example of where we were involved in our many visits back to the country. We travelled around extensively, attending and speaking at various conferences. We also became involved in a lot of leadership training alongside another Jubilee elder, Dave Adams, who, with his wife Herma, also became great friends of ours. Our many travels and visits caused us to grow ever more in love with the country. We appreciated getting to know so many churches and enjoying the beauty of the scenery. In how many other countries would you be able to view whales swimming in the ocean and see a herd of elephants on the same day?

Vivid Memories

There are so many stories I can recall, but I include just a few of them.

On our very first visit, although apartheid was beginning to break down and certain laws which supported it had been repealed, it was still very evident in some areas. We saw beaches with signs that said, 'Whites Only' and different racial groups known as Whites, Blacks and Coloureds (mixed race) were supposed to live in their own particular areas. The State Schools were still strictly segregated, and white children were very obviously getting a superior education. Private schools were not segregated, and some wealthier Black and Coloured parents were able to send their children to these. Universities were not segregated, and some churches were still in practice segregated even if they claimed not to be. Graham, as the pastor of the Vineyard, fought very hard against any form of racial segregation, and Simon passionately followed that same direction in his ministry. At this time, Nelson Mandela had been transferred from Robben Island, where he had been imprisoned for many years and was now being held in Pollsmoor Prison in Cape Town. One afternoon I was in a car with a mother from the church and also her teenage daughter, who was attending a private school. We began to talk about the future of the country and Nelson Mandela's possible role. At one point, the teenager intervened to say, 'In my school, most of the girls don't know who Nelson Mandela is.' I was totally stunned, but it certainly revealed the success of the white government's control of what was being said through the media. I will always remember the pictures we saw on television back in England when Nelson Mandela walked through the prison gates of Pollsmoor as a free man and the jubilation in the streets as he was driven through Cape Town.

On a subsequent visit to Cape Town, Simon was on a sabbatical, so we stayed in the guest wing of his house while he and his wife, Lindsey, were away for about seven weeks. One afternoon I took a shower when, next thing I knew, I was woken up by Sue coming into the bedroom where I was lying wrapped in a towel on the bed with absolutely no memory of having the shower or coming out of it. For a few minutes, I was rather confused and thought we were in England, but gradually, the fog cleared, and I was thinking correctly again. It was a rather disturbing incident, but I waited until getting back to the UK to see my own doctor. He put it down to stress, but I didn't really accept that as I didn't feel I was stressed when it happened; in fact, we were rather enjoying ourselves being in Cape Town again. A couple of years later, Sue was reading the Saturday Telegraph, and she said, 'You need to read this.' She pointed to an article written by a medical doctor who had sought some advice from another doctor whom he greatly respected. He told her that he'd been for a swim and then 'came to' an hour or two later with no memory of what had happened in the intervening time. 'Ah,' she said, 'You are the person I've been waiting to talk to!' She told him that there was a recognised syndrome in France when people suffered a total loss of memory for a short time, that it was always associated with water and never happened to the same person more than once. He was happy with that, and so was I. In more recent years, I have talked with another NewFrontier's pastor who told me that he went for a swim and then suffered a total loss of memory for some hours. He took time off because of it. I told him the above story and said, 'Well, it probably won't ever happen to you again!'

More disturbingly, one Saturday morning in early January 2005, Terry Virgo rang me and simply said, 'Simon Pettit is dead.' Simon had been on a ministry trip to a church in New Zealand. He had given some teaching to the church at a Saturday morning seminar before going outside for a break and to kick a ball around with some of the guys when he dropped dead of a heart attack. This was an immense shock. Simon was only 50, and his loss was felt by thousands. Besides his wife and family, there was the Jubilee Church, the whole NewFrontiers movement of churches, among which he was one of the best-known leaders, and multiple other churches he had contact with in southern Africa as well as in New Zealand and Australia. A few months earlier, he had handed the leadership of Jubilee over to a younger man, Steve van Rhyn, who was married to Terry's daughter Anna. Steve was still leaning heavily on Simon's wisdom and experience, so it was a huge adjustment for them as well. Simon's life and ministry are well remembered by many people years later.

A later visit took us back to Cape Town to cover a preaching series on Heaven while Steve was on sabbatical. I've covered some ministry for the sabbaticals of 3 Jubilee leaders! On a day off, we visited the famous Cape Point, often thought of as the most southerly extremity on the African continent – though, in fact, Cape Agulhas along the coast is still further south. But the Indian and Atlantic Oceans meet at Cape Point, and the views and scenery are quite stunning. Whenever we visited, we kept an eye open for baboons that roamed quite freely in the area. They are truly scary animals with very big teeth. That afternoon we were aware of a lot of baboons nearby as we drove into the car park. I headed for a space that looked baboon free and got out of the car, leaving the door slightly ajar. Within a couple of seconds, a baboon had opened the door, sat in the driver's seat and was rifling through the shelves looking for something to eat. Of course, Sue was pretty terrified and was struggling to get her door open, which, for some reason, was stuck. She fell out just as a security guard arrived with a big stick, and the baboon made a hasty exit. Whenever I've told this story, there is always someone who manages to ask how Sue knew it was a baboon and not me.

The Long Visit

I was approaching retirement, and a few people had contacted me asking whether I would consider being involved with their church. I had been invited by my friend John Wilthew who was leading a church in Northumberland, to bring some teaching there, and during our visit, he took me to a pastor's fellowship meeting in Newcastle. At the close of the meeting, the pastor of the Newcastle Church said that he had a picture for me. He had seen me holding a box of Smarties. As a man with a lifelong passion for Smarties, I was all attention. I had a choice of eating a blue or a pink Smartie. The blue one represented a safe choice, but the pink one represented a more risky choice. I should take the pink Smartie. Immediately John's son, Phil, who has a strong prophetic gifting, approached me and said that he believed that I still had another country in me. Naturally, I asked, 'Where?' but he didn't know! Neither comment made much sense. All approaches to me represented extremely safe choices, and I hadn't given a thought to going overseas in retirement. Two weeks later, Steve van Rhyn rang me from Cape Town to share that they were short-staffed on the eldership team and, as I knew their scene so well, would I consider going over to South Africa for the first year of our retirement? A couple of weeks after I had retired, we were back in Cape Town.

It was a very memorable year. I often refer to it as my 'gap year' – it's just that it came at the end of my working life rather than at the beginning, unlike most people. In the first couple of weeks of being there, we had a very unnerving experience. We had decided to drive up the West coast outside of Cape Town and look at the spring flowers, a famous spectacle in the early South African spring. On our drive, we discovered a garden which we paid to go into, where the spring flowers were just glorious. Walking around, we were approached by two teenage boys and another lad of about 11; they were obviously poor and asked us for money. I should have realised immediately that they wouldn't have paid to get into the garden and, therefore, could be likely to cause trouble, but rather than be careful, I just shooed them away. Maybe fifteen minutes later, we were in a very remote part of the garden, a valley area with no one around, and suddenly there were the three boys again. I knew we were in trouble. What happened in the next two minutes was a bit confusing, but they asked again for money and then added, 'All your money and your credit cards.' I shouted at Sue to run and stood in front of her while trying to pass small coins to the youngest boy to keep them away from us. Suddenly I realised that the oldest boy was holding a large rock right over my head and holding out his other hand. At the same time, Sue, not seeing this started to lecture the other two boys loudly – 'how dare you threaten us like this....' An unseen but well-built gardener some distance away saw and heard what was happening and began to run towards us. The boys then realised that they were in trouble and fled, although the gardener caught the youngest one, and the police were called.

I've often wondered whether the boy with the rock would have smashed it into my head. I've also always been grateful for my wife's grandmotherly lecturing and the 'angel' that rescued us.

It was a busy year with a lot of preaching and teaching in Jubilee and visits to numerous other churches. We also squeezed in a visit to Dubai to support the new leader of the church there and a ministry trip to teach Eschatology to leaders in Zimbabwe, which also gave us the opportunity to visit Victoria Falls. We returned home just before my 66th birthday, took a short break in Cornwall, sat overlooking a favourite beach and gave thanks to God for his grace to us.

After 20 years of regularly visiting South Africa, we've never returned. Sadly, I don't think we ever will.

Chapter 11

NewFrontiers

I can well imagine that there will come a time when someone will do some careful research and write a history of NewFrontiers. I have been involved for about half of my life, and my comments and perspectives are personal observations rather than the result of such research.

When Terry Virgo's ministry was beginning to draw a number of churches together and needing a name mainly for practical reasons, the group was called 'Coastlands.' This was inspired by Isa 42:4 'All the coastlands shall wait for his law, (NKJV). Although this speaks of an international vision, the fact that Terry was based in Brighton, on the south coast, meant that it might be misunderstood that Terry's ministry was restricted to seaside areas! The first time I was invited to a leader's meeting in Terry's home was before I left Moorlands Bible College, but it was the occasion when a change of name was being discussed. Sometime after that meeting, the name of 'New Frontiers' emerged though it was later contracted to 'NewFrontiers', a name that gave the feel of constantly wanting to break new ground and to advance wherever we could with the gospel and church planting.

There are some key distinctives that I've certainly always recognised as identifying NewFrontiers churches, and I will outline these here.

Evangelical. This is a word that can be used quite loosely today, but historically it has always referred to adherence to the Bible as the Word of God. Our desire has always been to build churches in a way that conforms to what we read in Scripture. This is a claim that may well be made by any denomination or group of churches. However, it would seem that, very often, churches have strayed from this ideal and no longer hold to that in practice. Of course, the challenge for us is to remain consistently biblical and not to ignore or compromise on what is clear in Scripture.

Charismatic. Years ago in Brighton, we took the opportunity to advertise our Sunday services in some of the local hotels. One of the elders asked me whether I thought we should describe ourselves as Evangelical or Charismatic. I replied that we could use both terms, but if we only used one, then it had to be Evangelical. My reason being that we are charismatic *because* we are evangelical. Our conviction has always been that the Holy Spirit is active in every generation. As there were clearly gifts of the Spirit used in and by the churches in the New Testament era, then we should expect the same today. Many of us who came from more traditional Christian backgrounds had to fight for this in the local church. Our argument was that we believed the Bible; spiritual gifts are taught about in the Bible with no suggestion that they ceased at a particular time; therefore, we are to seek and expect their manifestation today. That doesn't mean we adopt an 'anything goes' attitude - there is a right use of spiritual gifts. Indeed the right use of tongues and prophecy is something that Paul taught at length in his first letter to the Corinthian Church.

Reformed. This could be understood as meaning that our churches are Calvinistic, or to put it another way that we believe and teach, 'Once Saved Always Saved'. There is some truth in this, and we wouldn't want to deny it, even though some may struggle with it in practice. But more widely, to be reformed is to thoroughly embrace all that is meant by God's grace in the Bible. God initiates salvation, God calls us, God keeps us, we resist legalism, and we are eternally safe in Christ. In this teaching, we stand on the shoulders of men like George Whitfield, Charles

Spurgeon and Martyn Lloyd-Jones, but above all, it is because we see it in the Bible.

Kingdom. From its establishment, NewFrontiers emphasised the Kingdom of God. We are not called to build inward-looking fellowships, however successful they might appear to be, but we are to be agents of God's will being done on the earth. We look to see his rule extend across the nations with the gospel, with signs and wonders and with compassion and service to those in need. Jesus was always teaching about God's Kingdom. He, himself, demonstrated the nature of that Kingdom. At his return, he will bring in the full expression of the Kingdom as he rules over a new heavens and earth. In many ways, we tried to engage with this through evangelism and social action. However, the latter got a particular boost when, at one leader's conference in Brighton, Simon Pettit, on a visit back from South Africa, preached a message under the title of 'Remember the Poor.' This was enthusiastically received at the time and led to a whole number of new initiatives in terms of care for the poor and powerless. Soon afterwards, a whole new ministry, now called Jubilee Plus, was launched to help NewFrontiers churches engage in Kingdom initiatives.

Complementarian. In brief, this refers to a conviction that the Bible teaches that men and women are equal in terms of salvation but have complementary roles to play within the created order. The aspects of this that are debated most strongly are a) within marriage, the husband ultimately has the responsibility to take the lead, and b) within the church this also carries through in that elders, who lead the church, are male. In our early days, we enjoyed something of a honeymoon period with this teaching for two reasons. One was that there seemed to be an appetite for accepting that in marriage, men should be willing to take a spiritual lead, to carry responsibility and that the wife was willing to give him her wholehearted support in this. Secondly, many of the early leaders had come from churches with a congregational form of government, but where the deacons had often been seen as a group who were to keep the pastor under control. Very often, these diaconates were dominated by women. Now it was understood that God raised male elders to lead the church without that kind of restriction. In the early days of our history, our churches looked and felt different to many others because of these convictions.

Over the years, life has become a lot less straightforward. We are living through a time when women's rights have been strenuously exerted, often rightly so, and anything that appears to teach that women are in some way not equal to men has been increasingly contested. We have sometimes had to fight very hard to keep our heads above water on this. For one thing, we have never taught that women are less equal to men, only that we have different roles. Neither have we taught that women could not lead or exercise authority, only that ultimate authority is given to husbands and elders. It may, however, be true that sometimes our theology has been better than our practice, and that can make us vulnerable. This is not the place for me to argue all this out in a detailed way, but it seems to me that men's headship in marriage, though sometimes attacked as abusive and patriarchal, is answered by one verse in Ephesians 5 where Paul says: 'Husbands love your wives, just as Christ loved the church and gave himself up for her.' (vs 25). Taking the lead and carrying responsibility in marriage has to be in line with that verse; otherwise, it is not biblical complementarity. When it comes to men as elders leading the church, then, the Bible makes it clear that there is a Godly order in church life so that women may be honoured, protected, respected and feel free to use their gifting in the local church. We are still grappling with thoroughly working this out, but we are seeking to be faithful to Scripture.

Moving forward

The number of churches in relationship with NewFrontiers has grown steadily over the decades, and growth demands change. Without attempting to approximate numbers, as these will change all the time, we know that there are many hundreds of churches in tens of nations that identify themselves with NewFrontiers. For some years, we published a magazine that was circulated around the churches and which gave Terry the opportunity to address a large number of people in print and also included news of what was happening around the world. I remember a Baptist Pastor who regularly received a copy speaking to me about the magazine and asking why we never had any problems! While we were growing, some of our churches were beginning to draw quite large congregations, and we saw increasing involvement in new nations. However, I suppose there isn't a great benefit in washing your dirty linen in public. There were churches that joined us and then left us, and there were some leadership failures, but there was a lot of Kingdom advance.

One of the ways our growth was obvious was through the Bible Weeks and conferences that were held. Starting with under three thousand at the first Downs Bible Week, our final gathering at Stoneleigh reached 28,000 attendees over the course of a two-week period as we could no longer accommodate everyone in one week. There was an increasing international feel about these Bible weeks as Believers joined us from other nations. This intensified again when we moved on to hold an annual Leader's Conference in Brighton called 'Together on a Mission' (TOAM). Some of the speakers at these conferences were always from other nations or working in other nations.

All this growth meant that a necessary degree of delegation was already taking place. In certain nations, where there were a number of churches working with us, there would be a senior leader overseeing the work but regularly in contact with Terry. In some nations where we were working with very few churches, the oversight might still come from the UK while waiting for a senior regional leader to emerge. This also began to happen within the UK itself; there were senior leaders taking oversight of a number of churches. At this point, the term 'apostle' was not regularly used for these senior leaders. Increasingly, questions were being asked as to how NewFrontiers was going to shape up in the future with the growth that was taking place.

Some of the questions arose because there was a concern that there should be greater clarity for a time when Terry, himself, was no longer leading. I remember one hilarious moment when David Holden was talking to the NewFrontiers leaders, and Terry wasn't present. He came straight to the point by saying that a lot of people were asking him what we would do if Terry died. David said, 'We'll bury him.' When the laughter died down, he did add that the men working closest to Terry were aware that the issue needed to be looked at. However, a great leap forward took place in a rather dramatic way.

At the TOAM Conference in 2008, a year before I retired and went to South Africa, Mark Driscoll, the leader of Mars Hill Church in Seattle, was the main guest preacher. Since then, he has become a controversial figure, and a lot has been written and said about what went wrong at Mars Hill. Before that, he had built a church of many thousands, but later on, there was to be a collapse of this work largely attributed to his controlling style of leadership. However, on his visit to the TOAM conference, he made two very significant contributions. One was that he caused a lot of leaders to rethink their use of buildings. Generally, with growing churches, the expectation was to buy or build ever bigger premises. In today's world, this can be cripplingly expensive and especially in the south of England. However, Mark's ministry meant that many began to consider other models. Basically, he suggested that we make the maximum use of what we already had before investing huge sums of money in very expensive building programs. This undoubtedly resulted in a number of churches deciding to introduce repeat meetings in the same building and also to the development of multi-site churches.

But the real drama came when at an afternoon meeting, Mark began to speak about a successor to Terry Virgo. He set it in the context of church movements honouring but also replacing their founding father. He also made suggestions as to how this should be done. Whatever people felt at the time (and there were some pretty strong reactions!), the detail was really worked out later. Terry admitted that discussions had taken place about what would happen when he was no longer leading, but it always tended to drop down the agenda until Mark Driscoll's intervention brought it right up to the top! Terry didn't agree with the suggestions that Mark Driscoll had made about how it should be done but did agree that it was time to do something.

At the TOAM Conference in 2011, Terry publicly commissioned about a dozen men to develop their own apostolic spheres with all those churches that were willing to be joined to them. Largely the shape of this was already in place. There were a number of senior leaders who were clearly demonstrating apostolic gifting by overseeing a number of churches. However, it wasn't totally straightforward, and in a way, rightly so. We had always insisted that we built the NewFrontiers movement of churches relationally. Therefore in some instances, there were churches that had been overseen by a senior leader, but when these apostles and their spheres became more clearly defined, they felt they would be better relationally joined to another apostle. Some churches took their time to decide, and some churches, having linked to one sphere, later decided to make a change. A number of the biggest churches decided to stay outside the process altogether, and some of them have since developed their own apostolic spheres. It might seem like an untidy process, but in a way, it was good because it was meant to be relational, not organisational.

Another way this could have been done would have been to recognise one person to replace Terry when the time came for him to retire. The general feeling was this would not have worked. The big question would have been who should replace Terry and who would command the confidence to take the lead of all these churches. The overwhelming conviction seemed to be that Terry had done absolutely the right thing and the multiplication of apostolic spheres would enable further growth.

Third Stream

Years ago, I put together some material for a talk I called Third Stream Christianity. I've given this talk a number of times to leaders. The term itself is not original to me; I've seen it used a number of times, usually with reference to Pentecostalism.

We can consider the Roman Catholic and Orthodox churches to represent one stream.

Roman Catholic church life can be traced very far back into the history of Christianity. In the West, we tend to be somewhat ignorant of Orthodox Christianity (e.g. the Russian Orthodox Church), although the claim is made that they can trace their line of ancestry right back into the New Testament age, something that other expressions of Christianity would contest. Nevertheless, it has a long history.

The second stream is the Protestant churches, which would not in any way acknowledge the Pope or Orthodox Church Patriarchs as having any authority or jurisdiction over their churches. They trace their origins back to the Reformation and would see their authority to be in the Bible alone and not in any person, such as the Pope.

It has then been suggested that the Pentecostal churches represent a third stream with their emphasis on the present work of the Holy Spirit. In my talk, I argue that this is too narrow a definition of the third stream, that there has always been such a stream and that you could trace its origins back to very early in church history. This third stream could be considered a 'restoration' stream that has again and again been represented in groups of Christians. These are Protestant in the sense that they saw the Bible as their only authority, that they have always called for a thoroughgoing return to, and restoration of, biblical teaching when even the Protestant churches have wandered away from it. Yet, in a way, they have also been more first-stream in their tendency to believe in the miraculous and supernatural. It can be argued that the Roman Catholics have often descended into pure superstition with their reverence for relics and weeping statues and the like; nevertheless, they have always held to a belief in the supernatural and the miraculous; I believe that NewFrontiers and other new church movements fall most naturally into this third stream. Our strong conviction is: let's do it like the Bible says. Let's not get into all the complications of formal church life with its committees and Headquarters but also let's be open to the supernatural and the miraculous.

There are third-stream groups in early history whose names are hardly known today, but names that many Christians will have heard of would be the Anabaptists and the Huguenots. These groups have usually had a comparatively short lifespan. The reasons for that aren't hard to discern. Sometimes in their reforming zeal, they have become fanatical and really destroyed themselves – thus, the Anabaptists. Sometimes they have been persecuted out of existence by one of the other streams; that's true of the Huguenots. Sometimes leadership infighting has brought them down.

I doubt if fanaticism will destroy us, and I do not think that persecution will finish us off (though standing for biblical truth isn't as secure a position as it used to be). I think it unlikely that we will disappear because of leadership conflicts, for we now have a number of men recognised to have an apostolic calling and overseeing different groups of churches. Maybe our greatest danger is that we could simply lose our reforming zeal and cease to be part of the radical third stream. Indeed I've sometimes wondered if God raises up groups like ours for a time to help ginger up the rest of the church. If we lose our passion, God can always raise up another group, as he has done previously.

No one can confidently predict how our movement of churches will progress or decline in the future. But the Bible assures us that Jesus will build his church. With or without NewFrontiers, that will most surely be true.

Chapter 12

Leaders

During the course of a long ministry, I've had the privilege of interacting with many leaders. Sometimes I have listened to them; sometimes, I've taught them; sometimes, I've had conversations with them; and very often, I've laughed with them. One of my leadership convictions is that in the greatest crisis, there is always something to laugh about. Years ago, I was overseas and sitting with a church leader in a hotel drinking coffee as we had a fairly intense conversation. He came from the UK but was now leading a church in another country where a whole number of difficulties had arisen. We were talking through these and trying to discern a way forward. Suddenly, he leant across the table, looked straight into my eyes and said, 'John what do you really think I should do?' I replied, 'Get on a plane and go home.' At this point, we both burst out laughing. It broke something in the rather heavy atmosphere we were both feeling. It got better after that, we largely resolved the issues, and he went on to have a really successful ministry in the church.

Disappointments

Every year I hear of leaders who have fallen and had to leave their ministry. Some of these falls are very high profile and become widely known throughout the Christian world. This is incredibly damaging to the Body of Christ worldwide. I have been genuinely shocked and disappointed by some of the failures that have been revealed. Years ago, I was on sabbatical in America, and I stayed for a time with some friends who belonged to a 4,000-member mega-church. In the next few years, it grew to about 10,000. Pastors always want to know how another Pastor has achieved this sort of growth. In this case, it was largely attributed to the structure of the small group program, which had drawn in many unbelievers who had come to faith and joined the church. My visit happily coincided with a leaders' conference that was being hosted at the church; Sue and I were enthusiastic attendees. One of the issues that received a lot of attention was how the church was dealing with increasingly liberal views on homosexuality. Because of the size of the church, they had got caught up a few times in some complex situations with this, but they explained how they handled it and held to the traditional Christian position on this subject. The pastor was very clear and very passionate in his teaching on this. Some years later, I was listening to the BBC main news when there was a report given of how this same pastor had just resigned from his church in America after it was revealed he was engaged in a homosexual relationship. That was a real shock.

It's commonly stated that the three things that bring down leaders are sex, money and power. Sex seems to be the big one, though it may be that sexual failures tend to get more publicity than the other two. One thing I have noted about sexual failures, and I have taught this often to leaders, is that it seems to happen among older men, not younger ones. I think it would be easy to assume that it's younger leaders that would fall in this area. I find it very difficult to think of any leaders in their twenties and thirties that have fallen, but once men get into their forties and even more into their fifties and even sixties, then unfortunately, I could name many, too many, who have succumbed to sexual sin. I once wrote a blog about this that caused quite a strong reaction. I suggested that maturer leaders who fall into sexual sin may, in fact, be committing ministry suicide. What provoked me to think like this were some well-known casualties. The size of and respect for their ministries was so large: I couldn't understand why they would risk throwing it all away. Was it because, deep down, they wanted an exit route? The pressure on some leaders is relentless. Always having to preach great sermons, give excellent teaching, and to deal with constant streams of invitations where their ministry or endorsement is being sought. I wonder if the strain sometimes becomes so intense that they simply want out. But how do you get out? The quickest way is to commit suicide of sorts. So you enter into an affair which at the time probably seems both enjoyable and exciting, but you know that if you are found out, you are immediately gone, and it's all over, which could seem quite a relief. One pastor friend thought my view was very Freudian! But I also had a response from a Christian agency saying they were looking at this subject in a similar way themselves and asked me for some further comments.

The second pitfall is money. I have worked with a couple of leaders who were gifted men but got themselves involved in financial indiscretions that meant they had to stand down from leadership. In this area, there are shortfalls in financial integrity that can be hidden from view. I think particularly of how easy it is to preach up a storm about generous giving and yet not be generous oneself. It is easy to convince ourselves that our own financial pressures are uniquely challenging and make ourselves the exception to what we are preaching to others.

Thirdly, the misuse of power is usually seen in leadership difficulties in an over-controlling attitude towards others. Unfortunately, I have come across this a number of times. Leaders often have strong personalities, which is partly why they have made it into leadership. So it's not perhaps surprising that sometimes there are abuses in this area of control. At the same time, we are living in a culture where people can be supersensitive in these kind of areas. Today, people are encouraged to 'be themselves.' We are told nobody can tell us what to do or what to think. In the church, it's easy enough for elders who are pastorally interacting with individuals to be accused of control and manipulation. Clearly, it sometimes is, but I think it's also possible to be too quickly offended. However, elders can get out of touch, not listen to people properly, become intimidating in their attitude to others and produce a climate of fear. Leadership, as taught in the New Testament, is servant leadership, and Paul encourages us in Philippians to have the same attitude as Christ. Lord of all, yet servant of all. (Philippians 2:5-11)

It is often suggested that the best way of dealing with these leadership challenges is through accountability. We need to have those around us that can speak into our lives. I don't doubt for a moment that the 'wounds from a friend can be trusted' (Proverbs 27:6), but it's not the complete answer. I've known men who have belonged to a 'tight' accountability group where all the members have been very open with one another about their lives, but then one of them has simply lied. The Bible tells us to watch our lives and doctrine closely (1 Timothy 4:16). We have to be self-accountable, knowing that everything we do is happening before God, who sees all things.

When we talk of those who are qualified to lead in the church of God, it is common to identify character, gifting and anointing. Character is surely most essential because if that goes, then everything goes. However, someone may have great character but simply lack gifting in a leadership capacity. You don't want to listen to a preacher whose life is beyond reproach, but when you hear him, you lose the will to live! When it comes to anointing, I think the best definition I ever heard of this was: You know if you haven't got it.

Having written somewhat negatively about this, I think, thankfully, that most Believers, most of the time, are blessed with leaders who though being far from perfect, do display a measure of character, gifting and anointing that is a real blessing to those they oversee.

Three Leaders

I'm going to describe some leaders I have worked with over the years. Probably none of these will ever be well known across the Christian world, but they are examples of so many who serve faithfully and lead with great integrity and therefore know the loyalty and love of their people.

I met John and Jo Way when I first preached at Swalecliffe Free Church (Baptist). I was wanting to move on from my first church, where we had some bruising experiences, but where I had been baptised in the Holy Spirit and begun to enjoy a much richer understanding of the local church as the Body of Christ. I remember standing in their kitchen, helping with the drying up after they had given me lunch following the morning meeting. As we talked together, it was obvious that we were on the same wavelength. They had enjoyed a fresh encounter with the Holy Spirit and clearly felt there was a fuller expression of church life than they had enjoyed so far. We began a friendship then, which has continued for nearly 50 years as I write this. I don't think I've ever met a couple so committed to serving others as John and Jo. John worked for the Post Office as it was known then and commuted every day to central London. He was a church deacon and utterly supportive. Despite a heavy work schedule, he was nearly always present at every evening event midweek, and he once said to me about attending church on Sunday, 'If necessary I'd crawl across broken glass to be there.' He was very gifted with anything to do with house maintenance and repairs. He helped us frequently in that way. He was able to service a car, and when we first knew him ran a Rover 90 (old, even then), keeping it in mint condition. We bought it off him after a few years. It was the most beautiful car, but it only did 12 miles to the gallon. I ran out of petrol several times as I simply couldn't believe we'd used it all. On one occasion, I was rescued at the side of the road by a group of nuns who were driving past and stopped to give me a lift to a nearby garage. He was also musically gifted, a very competent drummer and for some years, he occasionally played for a well-known gospel singer at the time, Betty Lou Mills. Most helpfully for our church worship as it developed, he was also an excellent guitarist. As our worship began to change, it was John who really led the charge in introducing new worship songs and a much freer expression of worship. John was utterly reliable, and his wife Jo cared for and served people very sacrificially. At the age of 50, and after we had moved on, John was able to accept a redundancy package from his job which meant that he never had to return to secular work. For him, of course, this was the opportunity to give himself even more fully to serving the local church. Later still, when it was decided to plant a NewFrontiers church in Herne Bay, a small town just three miles away, John was asked to take the lead elder position. Even when he passed the lead over to someone else, he continued to serve as an elder and lead the church in worship. If there was something to be done in the church, you could guarantee that John and Jo would be there to do it. They had two sons, and very sadly, the older one died of cancer in middle age. Despite this real tragedy, they never faltered in their faith. Their younger son moved to live in Japan, so their contact with him is mainly limited to Facetime and just the occasional visit either way. I think, in many ways, they've had quite a tough life, but I also know from what they've said they don't see it that way at all. I have huge admiration for this couple. John has been an outstandingly faithful leader. He may never be well known, but for me, John and Jo are real heroes of the faith.

I got to know Ranjit on my first visit to India when after my adventures in the monsoon in Bombay (Mumbai), I flew down to

Goa. There were just one or two churches in Goa at the time that had linked to NewFrontiers, and the leader of one of them had established a residential training program for young men and married couples who might be church leaders in the future. Among them was this young man with a very sharp brain and rather English sense of humour called Ranjit. He was already making a big contribution to the local church in Goa. Later he became an elder and then, after a few years there, went on to lead it. For ten years, I had a two-week teaching slot with these trainees, and initially, we met in a flat the church had purchased at the top of an apartment block. It was basic, rather hot and sticky in the Goan heat, but it was a decent enough place to meet. Sometimes we ran out of water that then had to be carried up the stairs to where we met. The food was simple but spicy, and I struggled a bit; especially when I got a stomach bug. On my final day there, on my first visit, a young wife on the course asked me what I'd really like to eat. I ordered fried eggs and chips, and it was the best I'd ever had! I taught a number of subjects over the years, including The End Times and New Testament books. Ranjit was always on the ball and knew how to ask intelligent questions and make us all laugh at the same time. As a child, he'd caught polio; the vaccine was not freely available in that part of India at the time. It left him with a physical disability, and I think of times he must have found it very hard work climbing the stairs to the training base, but one thing that Ranjit has never done is to complain. India is a country where Arranged Marriages are common, and they had an interesting slant on this in the church. The senior elder would ask a young man if there was a young woman in the church that he felt drawn toward for marriage. The elder's wife would ask a young woman about her interest in any of the young men. Of course, the two had never talked to each other about this, but it was surprising how often it was discovered in this way that there was a mutual attraction. That is how Ranjit and Cynthia came to be married, and I think it's a very romantic story. Ranjit clearly had an outstanding preaching gift which has blessed not only his church but many other churches in India and overseas, including Portugal. Goa used to be a Portuguese colony, so this is rather neat. Being a Christian leader in India has its challenges, and the whole culture has turned more anti-Christian over the years. Ranjit and Cynthia, who was pregnant at the time, were once critically ill with malaria. He has travelled widely in India, obtained a doctorate and has served his own church for decades with utter faithfulness. Ranjit's spirit of endurance has been a huge example to me. He always speaks to me with great respect and says how much I've taught him. In reality, I think I may have learned more from him.

For just a couple of years at Brighton, we ran a full-time course that trainee leaders could attend for a year. The numbers were small, but one of those who attended was Stuart Radley. He also lodged with us for the year. When he first arrived, he had some inclination to work in North Africa, and he also spent a year in Paris, which enabled him to learn and speak French fluently, which would have been helpful in certain parts of Africa, but has also proved to be very helpful when he eventually planted a church in France! When he arrived in Brighton, he was already dating, but Sue always felt it wouldn't end in marriage and was convinced that he should marry an Algerian girl in our church called Amel, whose second language is French, and English her third language. I've always said that I think Sue put a hex on the first young lady, and the relationship came to an end, but it was a joy for me to take Stuart and Amel's wedding. By a wonderful coincidence, which I knew nothing about until I arrived at the meeting, I preached at their church in France on their 25th wedding anniversary. Stuart is a surveyor by training and established his own company in Brighton, but his heart was further south. Sue and I have had many holidays in France, and I was particularly attracted to Montpellier. I love the buzz of the city, its position near the south coast of

France and the fact that it has thousands of students. I said to Sue more than once that I thought it would be an excellent place to plant a church. When we returned from our year in South Africa, I met up with one of the Brighton elders who told me that Stuart and Amel had talked with the team and now, with their encouragement, were going to plant a church in Montpellier. Of course, I was delighted but wondered what he would do about his surveying business. The answer was that he would start by settling Amel and their three children in Montpellier and then would commute between that city and Brighton so he could still run his business. Over time the rhythm of this has varied a bit, but though Stuart is in Montpellier most weekends, he also spends a proportion of his time back in Brighton. The hope was that in the future, Stuart could be permanently working in France. He can't relocate his business there, and now, for more than a decade, he has worked both as a surveyor in England and a pastor in France. To say the least, this has been hugely demanding, but he has managed to build a church of about 100 people as well look after physical buildings back in the UK. I have huge respect for his energy and something approaching awe at the sheer determination and courage of someone who can run a successful business in the south of England and at the same time have a fruitful church planting ministry in the south of France. Again, Stuart may never be a widely known leader, but I have the highest respect for him and Amel.

In short, I've known of some very well-known leaders that have fallen. But I've known plenty of 'little known' leaders who have been wonderfully faithful.

Chapter 13

Bournemouth and Poole

The fact that I would soon retire really struck me seven years before it happened. While walking home in the early evening from our offices, the thought came like an unexpected revelation: I was now 58, and in a few years, my time as an elder in the Brighton church would be over. I was quite shaken and immediately began to think how I should best use those final years. About two years later, fellow elder Steve Walford was in my office talking to me about the way we should see the team shaping up in the future. Rather abruptly, he said, 'It's only five years and you'll be gone.' I remember at the time feeling slightly put out by the remark. I was being a bit over-sensitive, but perhaps similar feelings come to many men and women as they are approaching the end of their working lives. I did, however, remind Steve of this eighteen years later when he asked me to give a speech at his retirement bash. 'Now you're gone too Steve,' I said, which I'm sure he appreciated!

Three years later, a visiting leader from a London church said at our elder's meeting that perhaps it was right for me to consider retiring the following year. I felt it was the moment to seize the initiative and said I would be retiring at the end of June 2009. A few months before I did this, I rang Specsavers to book a regular eye test. I could only get there for a lunchtime slot, and the receptionist told me that they were always busy at that time, but I could have an appointment at a clinic on the first floor. She asked my age, which was then sixty-four, and then she said,' Will you be able to manage the stairs?' Suddenly I felt old and had to discipline myself from making a rather impolite response.

On the final Sunday that I preached as an elder at the Brighton Church, I asked to speak only in the morning and not at the repeat evening meeting as I didn't feel that I would have the emotional reserves to do it twice. That evening the team arranged a surprise farewell for Sue and me. Matthew and the family travelled up from Poole, and he hosted the meeting. Three of the granddaughters went on the platform to bring their greetings, and the other half of the family sent a video greeting from Chicago, where they were living at the time. Our one, very young grandson, managed a song of his own composition which contained one line with many repeats; 'Have a good day in your church.' Terry Virgo preached using the letters of the name Hosier as the heading for each of his points. With that, twenty-three years of ministry and eldership at the Brighton church came to an end.

We flew to America for a two-week summer holiday in Chicago with the family. Then it was back home to pack for our departure for the year in South Africa. Three months before our return to the UK, we had a message from Guy Miller, the lead elder of Citygate Church in Bournemouth. He invited us to move home and for me to join the eldership team there. We had previously had a couple of casual conversations about this possibility, but his invitation confirmed it. Our time in South Africa had loosened our ties with Brighton, plus Matthew and his family was in Poole, the town adjacent to Bournemouth where Matthew was leading Gateway Church. In fact, he had said to me, 'Move down near to us but don't join my church.' So everything seemed right for us to go!

Bournemouth

On arrival in Bournemouth, I immediately joined the eldership team at Citygate as a part-time volunteer and then stood down after six years before moving to Poole. However, I faced a major health challenge a few weeks after our arrival in Bournemouth. I have always been very proud of my good health and often told people that in 40 years, I'd only ever had to cancel two Sunday preaches because I was unwell. However, soon after we arrived, I woke in the middle of the night to go to the bathroom and suddenly, something clicked in my mind. Waking Sue, I said, 'I think I may have prostate trouble.' I had realised that my visits to the loo were becoming over frequent, and the next day, I was at the doctor's. He sent me for a blood test, and a week later, as I sat in his surgery, he told me that I had a high reading on the relevant test. It was at a level that might simply be due to my age, but that it could indicate prostate cancer. We were booked to fly to Australia a few weeks later, where I had been invited to run a Bible School for two months attended by a small group of emerging leaders coming from several countries in that part of the world. Should I now cancel that? My doctor told me that prostate cancer was typically very slow growing, so he felt that it would be alright to go, but then made it clear that it was my body and my choice. I went home very confused as to what I should do. Then I remembered that a pastor friend in Norwich had been diagnosed with prostate cancer about a year earlier and was still being treated for it, so I rang him that evening for a chat. He told me that his consultant was a member of his church. Would he like me to speak to him? Ten minutes later, he was back on the phone with the consultant's advice, which was not to go to Australia.

A couple of visits to a consultant in Bournemouth resulted in a biopsy on my prostate gland, and then Sue and I returned to see him a few days later. He only had to say, 'Unfortunately,' and I knew my life was about to change. The real shock came as he talked me through various procedures that would happen and then added that the next step was to have an MRI scan to check that the cancer hadn't spread to my bones. At that point, I froze inwardly because I was suffering from very severe aches in my left leg. We went home and, in one of the really low moments in our marriage,

I explained my pain to Sue and said that I thought that the cancer had already spread. During the rather sombre days that followed, we made a visit to Salisbury Cathedral, where there is a magnificent Baptismal Font (architecturally, not theologically!). Around its edge is inscribed Isaiah 43:2, *'When you pass through the waters, I will be with you; and when you pass through the rivers, they will not sweep over you. When you walk through the fire you will not be burned; the flames will not set you ablaze.'* Sue felt it was something of a sign for her and felt very comforted by it.

I had the MRI scan, and then in the worst two weeks of this whole experience, we waited for the result. But something else happened during this same time. Sometimes people talk about being carried by other people's prayers. During these weeks and on several other occasions, I had the experience of feeling as though I was literally being carried. It was quite extraordinary, and Sue felt it as well. We were sure people were praying. When I returned to see the consultant, he opened his file, looked at his notes and told me that the scan was fine. I was so taken aback that I asked if he was sure. He looked at his notes again and said, 'Yes, that's right, no trouble at all.' I felt I'd been given my life back, and a few days later, as the ache in my leg wore off, I realised that I'd probably had an attack of sciatica. The same consultant offered me either an operation or radiotherapy. I really wanted him to tell me what to do, but he insisted that either treatment offered an almost certain cure. Then he added, 'Whichever choice you make, when you've made it you'll have times when you'll think it was the wrong choice.' What to do? Sue said I should pray about it, which I thought slightly odd advice for a straightforward choice. But I did pray, and certain things began to happen that convinced me I should go for the operation. Half an hour after I had made a definite decision, my son, David, rang up from Chicago. He told me that they'd made good friends with a consultant there and that he'd talked to her about the choice I had to make. 'Tell him to have the op,' she said. It felt like a wonderful confirmation, and I never had a moment when I felt that I'd made the wrong choice.

Some weeks later, I had the operation and, at the time of writing, have lived eleven years since then without any further trouble. I have known so many men since who've also had the disease. It is the most common cancer in men and probably about the easiest to cure if caught soon enough. In recent years some well-known men in public life have spoken publicly of having the disease and urged men not to overlook warning signs, most commonly urinating more often. Sometimes there are no apparent symptoms. I had a friend some years younger than me whose wife urged him to go for a blood test. He had no symptoms at all, but his father had died of prostate cancer, and therefore his wife was concerned. By the time he had the tests, it had already spread too far to stop it, and sadly, he died. If there is a history of this cancer in the family or any symptoms, men are very foolish if they do the typical thing of delaying to see their doctor.

After recovering from my operation, we were able to enter fully into church life at Citygate. I was immediately involved with the regular preaching ministry as well as travelling to a number of other churches some Sundays. Guy was now overseeing an apostolic sphere which was given the name: 'Commission', and was working with a number of churches in the UK as well as Portugal and India. Once again, I was asked to be involved in Leadership training, and we established a base for the Advanced course alongside the Foundations course, which was already being hosted at the Citygate Church. I exported a mini version of the Advanced course to Portugal and visited there several times.

We also had a building program! Having been through that for over a decade at Brighton, I wasn't overexcited about repeating the experience, but at least my history there was of some benefit to what was happening in Bournemouth. The church had been fortunate enough to be renting a warehouse for the Sunday meetings when a builder offered to build a new church premises for free. The project was incorporated into a residential student block, and we had to pay for the fitting out at the cost of over a million pounds, which I thought sounded like a lot of money. But when I first walked into the new building, it was simply an empty shell; nothing had been put into it at all. The church raised the money on a mortgage, paid it off fairly quickly, and the work was done.

However, I still had another church-building program to face. And so we move a few miles along the coast to Poole.

Poole

In an earlier chapter about my time at Moorlands Bible College, I wrote about my involvement with Alder Road Baptist Church. I had worked with the church during my time in the College when they were without a lead pastor. Before I left, Phil Campion was asked to take that role. Because I was moving on to Brighton, it had sparked some interest among the church leaders at Alder Road about NewFrontiers. Over time they developed a relationship with local NewFrontiers' leaders and joined the movement of churches. I visited a few times, but the link gradually faded. Twenty years later, Phil moved to Pastor another church, and I received an invitation to go back and preach. I was unenthusiastic. It was the summer holidays, so I knew people would be away. It was a long round trip to drive, and I sensed that they would want to ask my help about a new leader, so I didn't really feel I would have anything to offer them. But I went, and the Sunday morning was very encouraging, with more people present than I had expected and a responsive congregation. So when I met with the elders afterwards, I was feeling a lot more positive. They did, indeed, ask me if I could recommend anyone to come and encouraged by what I had seen, I said that as I travelled to all the training bases, I would keep on the lookout to see if I could spot anyone who might be interested in coming. At the time, Matthew was on the move from Sidcup, where he had been leading the team there, but seemed to have another church in view. So I said to the Alder Road team that if they wanted a good preacher to visit while they were still looking, then Matthew would probably have a free Sunday, but it seemed that he was already in conversations about moving to another church. Matthew was invited to Alder Road to preach, and, as they say, the rest is history: in a short space of time, he accepted the invitation to become their Pastor.

When we moved to Bournemouth and joined the Citygate church; Sue and I were already discussing that the day would come when we would almost certainly move to Alder Road. As it happened, our house was exactly equidistant from the Bournemouth and Poole church buildings. Time passed, Alder Road became Gateway Church, and I served on the Eldership team at Bournemouth for six years. In standing down from that role, we knew it was the time to plan for our move to Poole. We didn't want to go immediately as it could have looked as though we had fallen out with Citygate, which we certainly hadn't and very much enjoyed being a part of it. After another year, we felt it was time for us to be with the family. Russell White, who was now the Citygate Leader, was very gracious to us about moving on. It was with some real sadness and expectation that, after seven years of turning right to drive to Citygate, we turned left to drive to Gateway. I had been in church leadership for nearly 50 years, and as I walked into Gateway that first Sunday, I realised that was never going to be my role again; we took seats near the back and applied for church membership.

During Matthew's time at Gateway, the church had grown, and they had run repeat meetings for a season. Later they decided to restructure the church into two sites. They returned to one meeting in the Alder Road building but planted a new congregation in a fish and chip shop in Poole. From there, they moved to a steak bar; then to a hotel and with another move, they had the use on a Sunday morning of a historic but crumbling Congregational Church near Poole Quay. Then a redundant Methodist Church building came on the market, but to secure, it required the congregation immediately to raise a third of the cost, which came to £100,000, and it was August. Matthew had faith for it. The church responded. The building was purchased. Situated at 502 Ashley Road in Poole, it's always referred to simply as 502.

Back at the Alder Road site, there were over-ambitious plans for a rebuild. Yes, another church-building program. The roof of the main building was leaking, and the church hall had been barely serviceable for decades. There had been many plans and false starts in an attempt to rebuild. Shortly after our arrival, yet another plan was agreed upon, which involved repairing the main building and redesigning it for children's and youth work while the old hall would be pulled down and a new meeting room erected for our Sunday meetings.

Then Covid struck. Obviously, this caused a delay with our building plans. Like other churches, we had to adapt to the lockdown regime. For a time, all our meetings took place on zoom with an elder playing the guitar in his house and Matthew preaching from his house. We moved on to live streaming a meeting from the Alder Road building with just a worship band and preacher present in the building. Then when things opened up again, we had a long season of reduced congregations spread over three meetings. Matthew would preach at Alder Road, drive to 502 to preach there and then back to preach again at a second meeting in Alder Road. Meanwhile, we could only be present by sitting far apart and wearing a mask. We weren't even allowed to sing, but somehow there was quite a loud volume of song – it must have been angels. Matthew decided that with all the disruption caused to the church by Covid, it would be best not to return to our normal pattern but to embrace another disrupted year by beginning the building program. We moved to repeat meetings at 502, and the builders began their work at the Alder Road site at the beginning of 2022 with a view to completing all the work by the end of the year. Having been through two previous church building programs, my faith level for opening the new premises was about Easter 2023. The builders were excellent. Despite the shortage of supplies and workers largely due to the ongoing effects of Covid, they kept to schedule, and we opened our new building on January 1st. 2023, crowding both congregations into the building for a great celebration.

Just before the building was completed, Matthew informed the church that, at the beginning of September, we had been victims of a fraud that had emptied our church bank account, which because of building fund money, was over half a million pounds. The elders, church treasurer and trustees had known about this, and it had put them under considerable strain. After some months of discussion, the Bank had refunded the entire amount. I've been through three major church-building programs. Each one had demanded faith on the part of church members. There have always been battles, but always victory, for though we have trouble in this life, Christ has overcome the world.

Chapter 14

Finishing well

Years ago, I read a book called 'Finishing Strong' by Steve Farrar which profoundly affected me. Right at the beginning of the book, he writes about three highly gifted American evangelists who came to prominence in 1945. One of them was Billy Graham. The other two were Chuck Templeton and Bron Clifford. Of those three, the author suggests his readers have probably only heard of Billy Graham. And that's the point. Chuck Templeton was initially better known than Billy Graham, and some saw him as the most gifted young preacher in America at the time. Bron Clifford drew huge crowds to hear him preach. So what happened to them? Templeton left the ministry to become a media commentator and later left the faith. By 1954 Clifford had ruined his life with alcohol and bad financial management; he'd left his wife and family and died at the age of 35. Farrar writes: 'In 1945, three young men with extraordinary gifts were preaching the gospel to multiplied thousands across the nation. Within ten years, only one of them was still on track for Christ.'

I've often read the opening section of this book to groups of young leaders when teaching about character. I always say to them that I'm doing it quite deliberately with the thought that if in years to come they are feeling tempted to walk away from their ministry or the faith, then they might remember I once read this to them and might think again. For me, there has always been a strong desire to finish well. Of course, some men leave a ministry but continue strong in the faith, but there are those who, sadly, fall away from both. I occasionally said to the congregation at Brighton that if, at the end of my ministry, all that people could say about me was that I'd loved my children, I'd been faithful to my wife, and I had never cheated on the church in any way, then I would be content with that. I had one emotional moment when preaching my final sermon as an elder when I repeated that to the congregation and received a warm round of applause. For me, it's really important not to finish famous, but to finish well.

Looking Back

I think reflection on the past is inevitable at the end of your working life and into retirement. Because I have been a preacher for so much of my life, I tend to look back through that filter. I consider myself fortunate that I never had a day when I was unemployed and that throughout almost all of my adult life, I was involved in Christian ministry. I felt a particular call on my life to preach, and that's what I did most Sundays. I believed my contribution was to be to explain God's word as carefully and as clearly as I could and to work hard at making the more challenging parts of the Bible accessible to others. I also felt a particular call to try and strengthen Believers in their faith as I preached the Word of God. Paul once wrote, 'Night and day we pray most earnestly that we may see you again and supply what is lacking in your faith.' (1 Thessalonians 3:10). It was that desire to supply what was lacking in other people's faith that I felt very strongly. Again, I responded to Paul's passion when he said, 'He is the one we proclaim, admonishing and teaching everyone with all wisdom so that we present everyone fully mature in Christ.' (Colossians 2:28). Paul wasn't satisfied just to see people saved; he wanted them to become mature disciples.

When I was coming to the end of my time at the Brighton Church, Joel Virgo invited me to preach for 3 Sundays in a row. Selecting a phrase from the Old Testament as my title, 'You will go out with joy,' (Isaiah 55;12), I chose three verses that had meant a lot to me over the years. There was some speculation as to what my final choice would be, and one of the elders guessed it right. In 1Thessalonians 3:8, Paul writes, 'For now we really live, since you are standing firm in the Lord.' It has long been my view that this is the most pastoral verse in the New Testament. I believe that much as a pastor wants to see people converted, he really gets his life seeing people stand firm in the faith. That verse in 1

Thessalonians will tell you if you are a true pastor. Evangelists get their life the other way round. Of course, they want to see people standing firm in the faith, but where they get their life is when people are saved. This helps to illustrate why we need all the different ministry gifts as they complement one another.

In retirement, I can see that my preaching ministry has gone into a slow decline in terms of how often I'm invited to preach. In my early retirement years, I was still preaching three times a month. Even then, it was interesting to see how often church leaders, whom I'd known well, would say to me, 'We must have you over to preach.' But there was no follow-up and no invitation that came through. Almost all the invitations that did come, though, were from leaders that I already knew, but for a variety of reasons, many of those leaders moved on from their churches, and so the link was broken. Invitations dropped to about two a month, and then came Covid. That seemed to break the links still further, and so invitations dropped to about one a month. I mention this because of the number of times I've been asked if I miss preaching. I find this a difficult question to answer. One of the things I recognise in myself are somewhat ambivalent feelings about preaching again in the churches where I've been an elder. Happily, I have been asked back to preach at all of them since leaving. It's very easy to feel that because you spent years of your life there that you have some kind of right to be invited back, but that's completely wrong. One is an elder in a local church for a season. When that season comes to an end, then it's entirely appropriate that others now preach there and hurt feelings about not being invited or nostalgic desires to return are not helpful.

I do have one slight regret about my very last sermon to the Brighton Church, though. Over a twenty-three-year period, I had preached there more than anyone, and after I'd retired, I spoke some four or five times again. But the very last time, to fit in with their current series, I was asked to give a sermon on hospitality. I've always wished I could have been given some grander topic to have spoken on. But then the danger is that I'm motivated by a desire to have finished by leaving some more memorable impression.

I've observed in some older preachers a feeling that they still have to preach every week, and they begin to drop hints about invitations whenever they can. I was determined never to do this. At worst, I think you can appear somewhat pathetic if you do. I've increasingly tried to appreciate over these years that I'm a member of a local church and have a responsibility to support it and be there regularly on Sunday. I'm not meant to be an occasional guest at my own church. I wonder if it's even possible to be more in love with preaching about the church than to love the local church. There comes a time when it is surely right to take a turn on the stewards or hospitality rota. So though I am still grateful to preach some Sundays, I do appreciate being an 'ordinary' member and taking my place alongside others in my home church. I felt that God said to me some years ago that it is time to Encourage, Support and Pray even if I was never asked to preach again. So in a way, I do miss not preaching as much as I once did, but in another way, I'm grateful to be among the congregation of my own church.

One subject I was asked to teach quite often during my ministry was preaching. I certainly believe one's ability to preach is more caught than taught or that it's a gift that is God-given more than a technique that can be learned. Nevertheless, it can be helpful to teach some guidelines that other preachers can think about, and a good way of learning is simply to listen to others who preach. Of course, the danger there is that you hook on to a favourite preacher and then consciously or unconsciously try to ape him. I once read a story of the first student that trained at the Pastor's College established by the great Victorian preacher C.H. Spurgeon. His name was Mr Medhurst, and when he was installed as the pastor of his first church, Spurgeon preached on that occasion. After the service, one elderly lady was heard discussing the service with another senior lady and remarking that Mr Spurgeon sounds just like our Mr Medhurst!

I believe it's important for everyone who is a preacher to have their own philosophy of preaching. It is very easy to think that preaching is mainly about conveying content to the congregation. A danger here is that preaching becomes more like lecturing. Early on in my ministry, I began to have doubts about this. These doubts grew when I started attending small groups that discussed the message from the previous Sunday. Very often, I found that the content hadn't been remembered, and when it was, sometimes it was misunderstood. There were even times when some of the content that was 'remembered' hadn't been in the sermon when it was preached. I found that my philosophy of preaching was articulated for me by an extract from The Puritans by D.M.Lloyd-Jones quoting Jonathan Edwards: *'It is objected that, when sermons are heard so very often, one sermon tends to thrust out another; so that persons lose the benefit of all.....the main benefit of preaching is by impression made upon the mind at the time, and not by an effect that arises afterwards by a remembrance of what was delivered. And although an after-remembrance of what was heard in the sermon is oftentimes very profitable; yet, for the most part, that remembrance is from an impression the words made on the heart at the time; and the memory profits, as it renews and increases that impression.'* Lloyd-Jones added: *The first and primary object of preaching is not only to give information,. It is, as Edwards says, to produce an impression. It is the impression at the time that matters, even more than what you can remember subsequently.'* (Pages 359-360). I believe that to be correct, so my hope and prayer have often been to bring people into an encounter with God through the Word of God at the time of the preaching. Incidentally, this underlines the importance of 'live' preaching. With so much preaching available online today, it can be assumed that to listen weeks, months or even years later is as good as being present at the time. Not so. There is something about the moment of preaching that is never recaptured later. Of course, content is also important. If you sit under faithful Biblical preaching week by week, a deposit of truth is built into your life to the extent that, very often, you know much more than you think you know.

Relationships

Just as my opportunities to preach have lessened, it also feels that my whole life has become gradually narrower as the years go by. I simply don't have contact with so many friends as I used to have. It's very easy to interpret this as other people not making contact with me as much as they used to. But I'm sure that I contact less people than I did in the past. I find it hard to be absolutely sure why this is so. Some friendships flourish simply because you are thrown together a lot. If you work on a team together then you can become good friends, but when the team breaks up, even for good reasons, then the urge to keep contact with some of the team members can fade. Is it true that we can be friends with someone as long as we gain some benefit from that person? If the benefit fades (say, they no longer ask you to preach at their church!) then once again the friendship can die away. So among all the elders I served alongside at the Brighton Church I retain strong connection with four of them, lesser contact with another four and very minimal contact with most of the others.

But as life narrows in terms of old friendships, there is more time for the family. We live very near one-half of the family and see them quite frequently. Our younger son and family live over 100 miles away, and we see them less often but usually for a longer time when we do meet up. Some years ago, I was invited to speak at a church on the subject of honouring parents as an adult. One of the matters this made me consider was our attitude to grandchildren. I don't think that parents realise the closeness of the bond that exists between grandparents and their grandchildren until they, themselves, become grandparents. Basically, your interaction with grandchildren can go through various stages; delight, fun, hard work, worry and pride. Live long enough, and even your grandchildren start to marry and carry off bits of furniture from your home!

One huge blessing is that my wife has shared not only my working life but also a long retirement. It's a cliché to say that you're so busy in retirement that you don't know how you ever found time to go to work. Part of the answer is that you have more energy when you are younger. But in retirement, you do have more flexibility. So although we've kept busy, we've also enjoyed a lot of relaxed times together. I am so grateful to have a wife who loved being an elder's wife, who fully supported my ministry (she says she kept me sane) and who gave so much of her time and energy looking out for members of the church and giving hospitality. I realise that some pastors have very few years of retirement to share with their wives and are quickly left as widowers. I have been so very fortunate that we have been able to enjoy many retirement years together.

What now?

During these years, I have preached several times what I call: End of life messages! The first one I simply called 'Forty years' and was fifteen brief reflections on my years as a pastor and included some things I would have done differently given my life again. I followed this later with: 'Convinced of this', a phrase ripped out of context from Philippians 1. In it, I spoke of things that I was convinced of when I began my ministry and remained convinced of to this day. These are my headline points:

I am convinced of this:

- Jesus is Lord

Other leaders come and go

- God loves me

I've had a lifetime to prove it

- The Bible is true

Historically so, but also by inner revelation

- The church is the hope for the world

133

Yes, Jesus is, but the church spreads the message

- We must keep the main thing the main thing

Many things are good in the Christian life, but above all, we need to know God

- We should be up to date

Be a church for today, not yesterday

- We don't compromise to our culture

But fight today's issues, and don't give in to the world

- The Christian life is a battle

It's not like a battle; it is a battle

- We have victory over death

Death is gain, or why bother?

- There is an end to this story

Jesus is coming soon

Particularly in the world of politics, I often hear mention of a desire to leave a legacy. Presidents and Prime Ministers want to leave a legacy by which they will be remembered. This can also come quite strongly into the church, and I do not believe it is always helpful. I have nothing against leaving a legacy, as such, and I'm grateful for that which others have left. I think of the writings of CS Lewis, the written down sermons of Spurgeon or the evangelical fruit of Lloyd-Jones's ministry. In the NewFrontiers family, I often think of Simon Pettit's early death, yet the legacy he left in terms of remembering the poor and how that still bears fruit in our churches. I am sure that Terry Virgo will leave a great legacy of a better understanding of grace for many or of a vision for a restored church which has so impacted my life and which I'm sure will impact the lives of many others. My concern is for individuals who seem agitated about leaving a legacy so they can be remembered. I do not think that is the point. We are surely called to serve God as fruitfully and faithfully as we can in our own generation, and whether or not we leave a legacy behind shouldn't be our concern; that's in the hands of God. I recently read this statement as a tweet: Preach the gospel, die, and be forgotten. I really respond to that. I'm not trying to be falsely modest, and indeed I am writing this book so that my family might have an account of my life when I have gone. But in the end, it's not for me to be concerned about my legacy or even worry if I'll be forgotten. Jesus is Lord, he saves, and he will bring his people to eternal life; that's what matters.

Epilogue

The Other Side of The Door

By its very nature, a biography looks back on life. But there will come a day when the door swings open, and we will walk into a fuller and richer life. I suppose because I have regularly taught about the End Times, people often ask me what will happen when they die. In this book, I have been writing about my life on this side of the door, but what about the other side of the door? No one's eschatology or view of the End is perfect, whether that be the end of history as we know it or our personal end. But there is a lot of information given to us in the Bible and especially in the New Testament to help us.

The Intermediate State

The main emphasis in the Bible's teaching about our eternal future is on when we receive a new resurrection body. However, it is obvious that when we die, we don't immediately receive that body. Our corpse is buried or cremated, and there is no longer a visible body. Most Christians believe that there will be a conscious existence even then. Theologians refer to this as the 'intermediate state'. When Jesus spoke to the dying thief at Calvary and said, 'Today you will be with me in Paradise' (Luke 23:43), that wouldn't be in a visible body as his corpse was disposed of following his crucifixion. In 2 Corinthians 5, Paul is clearly anticipating his resurrection body and speaks of the present body as a tent, which is fragile and easily destroyed. This is contrasted with the new body to come, which is likened to an eternal house which is clearly robust and solid. (2 Corinthians 5:1). He then goes on to speak of nakedness after death which is not really what he wants as he longs to be clothed with his new body, but then he concludes that even so, it would be better to be away from this body and to be at home with the Lord. (2 Corithians 5:8). So we can say about the intermediate state that we will be consciously with Jesus, and it will feel like we are at home. Even when we are away from home for only a few hours and having a tough day at work, we can long to get back home. We can enjoy a wonderful holiday, but we still feel glad that soon we will be returning home. The intermediate state will mean that we will feel at home, that it is the place where we belong and feel most comfortable. Jesus will be there.

The Final State

The main emphasis in the New Testament about the Believer's eternal destiny is on the final state. However long I may be in the intermediate state, that will be nothing compared to the eternity of our final state when Jesus returns. This is what I believe I will experience on the other side of the door.

All hope will be fulfilled. 'We wait for the blessed hope – the appearing of the glory of our great God and Saviour, Jesus Christ.' Titus 2:13 tells us whatever hopes we have now, the greatest hope is in the Return of Christ. Unlike other hopes, this one is different in the sense that it is absolutely certain that it will deliver. Other hopes may not be fulfilled, but this 'blessed hope' I will definitely see.

In 2Thessalonians 1:10 Paul writes of the wonder of Christ's return. He says: '… he (Jesus) comes to be glorified in his holy people and to be marvelled at among all those who have believed. This includes you..' I cannot conceive of the splendour and glory of Christ when he comes again. All peoples of the earth will see it, and many will weep (Revelation 1:7). But for all Believers, this will be an event we can only marvel at.

I will receive a new body. In some way, all of us find our present bodies unsatisfactory. For some, it will be because they carry some disability or disfigurement. But even for the most beautiful, their bodies will be a declining asset as they age, and perhaps the most beautiful are the most worried about what will happen to them physically. The Bible is very clear that when Jesus comes again, Believers will receive a resurrection body that is even likened to the body of Christ himself. (Philippians 3:20-21. 1 John 3:2)). We will never have to worry about our body again, which will never age, get diseased, suffer pain or die. I've always been fascinated by the fact that when Christ first rose from the dead, he was often not immediately recognised by those that knew him best but who were then overjoyed when they did recognise him. (Matthew 28:17. Luke 24:13f. John 20:11f). I sometimes imagine that in our new bodies, we will meet again those that we've known well and say' 'Is that really you?' They might reply, 'Yes, it is, and you've certainly improved!'

I will come before the judgement seat of Christ. (Revelation 20:11-15). As an evangelical Christian, I've constantly preached that we are saved through faith in Christ's atoning work and not at all by our works. However, our works as Christians do have significance. Here, in Revelation, as well as in other parts of the New Testament, we are told that there will be a judgement of our works, and the result of that assessment will not affect our salvation, that's already eternally secured, but it will affect our rewards. We always want to know what those rewards are. The New Testament gives some hints about this, and in 2 Peter 1: 11, we are encouraged to live in such a way as to receive a rich welcome into the eternal kingdom. I assume that this is a reward, and therefore we could live in such a way as to get less of a welcome.

I will attend the marriage supper of the Lamb. (Rev 19:6-9). The Church, which is the Bride, will celebrate her marriage to the Bridegroom, who is Christ. There are some who suggest that they'll be no food at this marriage supper because the description is metaphorical or picture language. For me, this underlines that there is a common viewpoint that somehow eternity will diminish what we enjoy now, probably to be replaced by one long Church service. Rather, we should see that what we enjoy now will be enhanced. We often celebrate by having a meal together and serving the best food. Think of Christmas. Think of a family wedding. We love to eat together on these occasions. Why should there be some lesser version of that in eternity? Surely the marriage supper then will be an increase and expansion of every celebration that we have on earth now. I am, however, pleased to think that there will be no hanging around for the photographs, but what a celebration it will be.

I will be an explorer. If we have new bodies, then we will need a new place for those bodies to live. The Bible, in both testaments, speaks of a regenerated creation and a new heavens and earth. (Isaiah 65:17. Revelation 21:1) We won't be living in some ethereal state of 'up there, out there, somewhere.' We will live on a reborn planet, earth. The blood of Christ is not only powerful enough to reconcile us to God but to redeem the whole creation as well (Colossians 1:20). Some suggest it was Mother Theresa of Calcutta who once said that if we can look back on our past life from the perspective of eternity our time on this earth will seem like one bad night in a second rate motel. However, we will live out our eternity in a new creation, and if all of it is going to be renewed, then it will be worth exploring. This is surely one of the implications of getting to grips with the infinite riches of Christ. (Ephesians 3:8). Have you ever wondered why the Universe is SO big? Surely it has to be big enough to be explored by those who are going to live forever. The riches of Christ demonstrated in the new creation will be boundless and inexhaustible. Besides that, we shall surely forever explore the wonder of salvation and the meaning and depth of the work of the Cross.

I will sing new songs. (Revelation 5:9). We are constantly singing new songs in praise of God upon the earth now. We have volumes of hymns that come from writers over the course of history. We might think particularly of Charles Wesley. Still today, in the twenty-first century, we raise our voices to praise Jesus with another new song that has just been written. When in eternity, we will know so much more about Christ and his work, we can understand that new songs will be composed forever.

There will be fellowship with all the people of God. In Revelation 7:9-11 we see that all the redeemed are gathered together around the throne of God and the Lamb and every people group is represented. Will I know the people I've been close to on earth? Most surely, I will. If eternal life means anything at all, it means I must know I exist. If I can recognise myself, I will surely be able to identify others that I have known. Moses and Elijah were given a visible form and made a guest appearance on the Mount of Transfiguration. They were recognised by the disciples who'd never even seen them before. We'll have such rich times with all the saints in their risen bodies who are gathered in from all the nations of the world.

I will see the face of God. (Revelation 22:4) To see the face of someone we love is one of life's greatest joys. Think of returning to a rail station or an airport after a long trip away. We strain to see the familiar face of someone who is waiting for us, ready to greet us. What joy when we do. The highest and greatest experience of all will be to see God's face, and he will recognise us because his name will be written on our forehead (Revelation 22:4). No wonder we will always be worshippers in a dimension which is beyond imagining.

One day the door will open, and we will be on the other side.